3800 11 002111

THE HIGHLAND CO

D1140313

A LOST LADY OF OLD YE.

JOHN BUCHAN led a truly extraordinary life: he was a diplomat, soldier, barrister, journalist, historian, politician, publisher, poet and novelist. He was born in Perth in 1875, the eldest son of a Free Church of Scotland minister, and educated at Hutcheson's Grammar School in Glasgow. He graduated from Glasgow University then took a scholarship to Oxford. During his time there – 'spent peacefully in an enclave like a monastery' – he wrote two historical novels, one of them being *A Lost Lady of Old Years*.

In 1901 he became a barrister of the Middle Temple and a private secretary to the High Commissioner for South Africa. In 1907 he married Susan Charlotte Grosvenor; they had three sons and a daughter. After spells as a war correspondent, Lloyd George's Director of Information and a Conservative MP, Buchan moved to Canada in 1935 where he became the first Baron Tweedsmuir of Elsfield.

Despite poor health throughout his life, Buchan's literary output was remarkable – thirty novels, over sixty non-fiction books, including biographies of Sir Walter Scott and Oliver Cromwell, and seven collections of short stories. His distinctive thrillers – 'shockers as he called them' were characterised by suspenseful atmosphere, conspiracy theories and romantic heroes, notably Richard Hannay (based on the real-life military spy William Ironside) and Sir Edward Leithen. Buchan was a favourite writer of Alfred Hitchcock, whose screen adaptation of *The Thirty-Nine Steps* was phenomenally successful.

John Buchan served as Governor-General of Canada from 1935 until his death in 1940, the year his autobiography *Memory Hold-the-door* was published.

JAMES ROBERTSON's novels are *The Fanatic, Joseph Knight* (recipient of both the Saltire Society and Scottish Arts Council Scottish Book of the Year awards in 2003/4), *The Testament of Gideon Mack* (long-listed for the Man Booker Prize in 2006) and *And the Land Lay Still* (which also received the Saltire Society Scottish Book of the Year award in 2010). He has also published two volumes of short stories, several collections of poetry, and many books in Scots for young readers. His edition of the *Selected Poems* of Robert Fergusson is published by Polygon. He is an honorary Research Fellow in the Department of Scottish Literature, University of Glasgow.

JOHN BUCHAN

A Lost Lady of Old Years

Introduced by James Robertson

HIGHLAND
LIBRARIES

10021116

Polygon

First published in 1899 by John Lane
This edition published in Great Britain in 2011
by Polygon, an imprint of Birlinn Ltd

West Newington House
10 Newington Road
Edinburgh
EH9 1QS

www.polygonbooks.co.uk

ISBN 978 1 84697 203 4

Introduction copyright © James Robertson, 2011

British Library Cataloguing-in-Publication Data
A catalogue record for this book is available on request
from the British Library.

Typeset by Hewer Text UK Ltd, Edinburgh
Printed and bound by CPI Cox & Wyman, Reading, RG1 8EX

Introduction

'A sneaking piece of imbecility' was how Sir Walter Scott privately described his young hero Edward Waverley, not long after the publication of *Waverley* in 1814. There is no record of John Buchan having applied any such dismissive epithet to Francis Birkenshaw, the protagonist of *A Lost Lady of Old Years*, but perhaps this is because Buchan does not spare him in the pages of the novel itself. If Edward Waverley is insipid and impressionable, he is also far too polite ever to be in danger of serious misconduct. Francis, on the other hand, is an angry young man with a tendency to violence. He has none of the honest decency of John Burnet, the hero of Buchan's preceding novel. Francis has fought his way through a rough childhood in Edinburgh 'inch by inch, wound by wound', and by the age of eighteen has knocked out a rival in love, stabbed a landlord, struck a woman, and tossed a would-be comrade into a ditch. There is plenty to suggest, as the narrative does, that he might 'grow to a blackguard of some quality'. When he turns his back on relative comfort and security for adventure he does so not for honour or romance, but out of selfishness: 'the only baseness seemed to lie in settling upon his lees in the warm air of the reputable. A hard conscience and a ready hand were a man's truest honour, and with this facile catchword he went whistling into a new life.'

Vital though the influence of Scott was on Buchan's development as a novelist, it is worth remembering that, in purely Scottish terms, more immediate precedence lay in the work of Stevenson, including his last, unfinished work *Weir of Hermiston*. That potentially magnificent, big-themed novel was published posthumously in 1896, in the middle of a decade which was the heyday of the sentimental and often parochial Kailyard school of writing; *A Lost Lady of Old Years* appeared in 1899; and two years later came *The House with the Green Shutters*, George Douglas Brown's vicious response to the Kailyard. The young Buchan was well aware that change was afoot in the world of Scottish fiction, and it could be said that Francis Birkenshaw picks his morally ambiguous way through a literary as well as a physical landscape.

Buchan was also learning from his own enviably prolific output. This was his third published novel and his seventh published book. He completed most of it when he was twenty-two years old and a student at Brasenose College, Oxford, and it appeared shortly after he celebrated his twenty-fourth birthday. His biographer Janet Adam Smith is unenthusiastic in her assessment: 'It is not nearly such a good story as *John Burnet of Barns*. We have to put up with the vacillations of Mr Francis Birkenshaw before we are caught up into any excitement of action, and Buchan's study of this romantic temperament is not keen or subtle enough to hold attention on its own merits . . .' This rather misses the point. It is the vacillations of Francis Birkenshaw, his swithering between idealism and self-interest, meanness and generosity of spirit, that make him interesting. True, some of the plotting is clunky – on one occasion a new character is suddenly introduced to get the author, it seems, rather than the hero, out of a tight spot – but while *A Lost Lady* may not be perfectly executed, its themes are handled with remarkable maturity and confidence by such a young author. Several of the hallmarks of Buchan's work are here – high adventure, scheming adversaries, a lonely man at large in wild country – but there is also a strikingly bleak view of human nature, where divisions between heroism and villainy, principle and compromise, youth and old age, are ragged and in some cases broken entirely, which has the ring of truth about it.

Another strand of authenticity is to be found in Buchan's mastery of Scots language, particularly but not exclusively in dialogue. His understanding of how eighteenth-century Gaelic-speaking Highlanders and Scots-speaking Lowlanders would have moved between different linguistic registers is also impressive. As always, too, his descriptions of weather and landscape are first-rate. This is a writer who listens and hears, who looks and sees. And there is that other aspect of Buchan's writing, the notion of 'the hurried journey'. 'We live our lives under the twin categories of time and space,' he wrote in the posthumously published *Memory Hold-the-Door*, 'and when the two come together we get the great moment. Whether failure or success is the result, life is sharpened, intensified, idealised.'

What better 'moment' in which to explore these ideas than the Jacobite Rising of 1745–6? The plot takes Francis Birkenshaw from the Lowlands to the Highlands, to London, and back to Scotland again. His physical route is matched by a journey towards virtue, a destination – like the settled, unassuming Fife town of Dysart where he ends up – to which his own nature seems not at all suited. The vision of a beautiful woman is at times his inspiration, at times his goad and torment; he sways between disgust and admiration as witness to the self-serving machinations of the old clan chief, Lord Lovat; and, still in his teens, he emerges from his experiences 'a grave old-featured man':

> A year ago he had been a boy; now he felt himself an ageing, broken man, driven in curb along a stony path of virtue, a man passionate yet austere, with a cold, scrupulous heart and a head the prey of every vagrom fancy. A man with great capabilities, truly, but scarcely a man to live pleasantly, at ease with himself and the world.

Virtue, sombre and mundane, is forced upon him, not won voluntarily by conscious endeavour. If *A Lost Lady* is cast in the mould of *Waverley*, the compromise between prudent head and impassioned heart is not nearly so comfortable in Buchan as it is in Scott. For Francis Birkenshaw, there is no room in the future for affection for a past, lost cause. As the novel closes, he declines the opportunity of adventures abroad, accepting that his lot is to return to 'the vulgarity of home'. 'I must bide in my own land, for I cannot flee from myself . . .' He receives no romantic reward for making this choice. Unlike Edward Waverley, Francis doesn't win the 'right' girl as a consolation for

losing the 'wrong' one. The conclusion of Buchan's novel is a
variation on Scott's, certainly, but it is delivered in a minor key.
All the moving scenes leading to the execution of Lord Lovat are
designed to show how a man must ultimately come to terms
with himself as he is, not as he might wish to be. In enclosing
this sobering message in a novel about the 'Forty-five, Buchan
may have upset the expectations of some of his readers. At any
rate, *A Lost Lady* was among his commercially least successful
novels, and has been unjustly neglected down the years.

It appears not to have been an easy book to write. 'The *Lost
Lady* has now reduced my hair to a silvery white,' he complained.
In a letter to his old friend Charlie Dick in February 1897 he
wrote, 'I have lately been reluctantly compelled to the conclusion that Mrs Murray of Broughton was really a very bad lot,
and that her life does not bear inspection. So I shall have to put
a note to my book saying that I have abandoned the historical
conception.' This indeed he did, in the dedication to Duncan
Grant Warrand, but he need not have apologised on this score.
His treatment of the historical figures, Duncan Forbes, Lord
Lovat and the Murrays in particular, is skilful and effective:
lightly sketched they may be, but – as with his wonderful
portrait of the young Samuel Johnson in his second Jacobite
novel *Midwinter*, written twenty-four years later – he has the
imaginative touch that marks a good historian as much as a fine
novelist, and shows them as human beings where a lesser
writer might have pasted them in as mere historical cut-outs.

Few names in Scottish history are as tarnished as that of John
Murray of Broughton. The year before the publication of *A Lost
Lady*, Robert Fitzroy Bell produced an edition of the *Memorials
of John Murray of Broughton*, a collection of his papers and
journals. In his introduction Bell makes a valiant attempt to
redress the balance of opinion in Murray's favour, but it feels
very much as if he knows he himself is fighting a lost cause.
Eventually he is reduced to slighting Mrs Murray in order to
cast her husband in a better light. While he was in the Tower of
London, Bell says, she deserted him for the continent, never to

return, and was subsequently 'unfaithful' to him. In a footnote, Bell mentions a tradition in the Murray family that she became Prince Charles Edward's mistress, only to add the qualification that there is no evidence for this. A strange defence indeed of Mr 'Evidence' Murray, as Jacobites referred to him after his appearance for the Crown against the Lords Kilmarnock, Balmerino and Lovat, but probably it is about the best Murray was likely to get, even so long after the event. For it was not only the Jacobites who despised him. Murray had become a Freemason when in Rome in 1737, and the following year affiliated to Lodge Canongate Kilwinning No. 2 in Edinburgh. Wherever his name or signature appear in the Lodge's transactions, they have been obliterated.

Then there is the story behind 'Broughton's Saucer', one of a number of 'out-of-the-way things' that the young Walter Scott collected while still living at his parents' house in George Square, Edinburgh. The story dates from around 1764 – seven years before Scott's birth – the year Murray, who had been living in London since his release from the Tower in 1747, sold the ancestral estate of Broughton for £16,000 to Mr Dickson of Ednam House, Kelso. Dickson's agent was Mr Scott, the father of the novelist. At this time the new development of George Square had not been built, so the following extract (from J.G. Lockhart's biography of Scott) presumably relates to an earlier residence, perhaps the one in College Wynd where Scott was born in 1771:

Mrs Scott's curiosity was strongly excited one autumn by the regular appearance, at a certain hour every evening, of a sedan chair, to deposit a person carefully muffled up in a mantle, who was immediately ushered into her husband's private room, and commonly remained with him there until long after the usual bed-time of this orderly family. Mr Scott answered her repeated inquiries with a vagueness which irritated the lady's feelings more and more; until, at last, she could bear the thing no longer;

but one evening, just as she heard the bell ring for the stranger's chair to carry him off, she made her appearance within the forbidden parlour with a salver in her hand, observing, that she thought the gentlemen had sat so long, they would be better of a dish of tea, and had ventured accordingly to bring some for their acceptance. The stranger, a person of distinguished appearance, and richly dressed, bowed to the lady, and accepted a cup; but her husband knit his brows, and refused very coldly to partake the refreshment. A moment afterwards the visitor withdrew – and Mr Scott lifting up the window-sash, took the cup, which he had left empty on the table, and tossed it out upon the pavement. The lady exclaimed for her china, but was put to silence by her husband's saying, 'I can forgive your little curiosity, madam, but you must pay the penalty. I may admit into my house, on a piece of business, persons wholly unworthy to be treated as guests by my wife. Neither lip of me nor mine comes after Mr Murray of Broughton's.'

'This was the unhappy man,' Lockhart continues, 'who, after attending Prince Charles Edward Stuart as his secretary throughout the greater part of his expedition, condescended to redeem his own life and fortune by bearing evidence against the noblest of his late master's adherents . . . The saucer belonging to Broughton's teacup chanced to be preserved; and Walter had made prize of it.'

Murray's betrayal, and the subsequent trial and execution of the Jacobite lords in London, fill some of the last pages of Scott's *Tales of a Grandfather*, which would have been a staple of John Buchan's early reading. The same episodes are played out in the later chapters of *A Lost Lady*, and are brilliantly done. The subtle conversations between Francis and, one after another, Duncan Forbes the Lord President, John Murray, and Simon Fraser Lord Lovat, serve to focus on the central theme, the fine line between honour and expediency, and between self-fulfilment and selfless devotion to a cause; on, in short, what permits individuals to live with themselves. Buchan deals angrily but humanely with Murray, and this is reflected in the moment when Francis contemplates murder as a means of silencing him:

> But the white, weak, unwholesome face deterred him. The man seemed worn with toils, seemed spiritless, friendless, and feeble. He could not draw upon him any more than upon a woman. With a cry of despair he turned upon his heel and left the room.

If Francis's view of Murray is grounded in contempt, his relationship with the devious, scheming but massively imposing Fraser of Lovat, whom he admires and despises almost in alternate sentences, is much more complex. Buchan's portrait of this complex, gross yet fascinating figure is superb, as the *New York Times* observed in its review:

> For its striking portrayal of Lovat this new Scots narrative is chiefly noteworthy. Crafty Simon Fraser's strange personality is depicted with a masterful touch. He is exhibited, in his old age, in many moods, violent, brutish, calm, and majestic. A traitor, a gourmand, a sot, a decayed débauché, he is also a scholar, a wit, a soldier, and a statesman. The Highlands never produced an odder character, while few of the Highland romancers have put a historical personage into fiction with greater power and picturesqueness. He has, almost, Gargantuan breadth of humour, Hogarthian strength of outline.

In Margaret Murray, the Lost Lady herself (the fine title is taken from Robert Browning's poem 'Waring') , the memory of whose tears drives Francis frantic before her feckless husband, Buchan fashioned another extraordinary character, this time from limited historical information. Robert Chambers' *History of the Rebellion in Scotland 1745–6* records the famous incident after the Highland army's entry into Edinburgh, when Prince Charles had his father proclaimed king at the Cross: 'During the ceremony, Mrs Murray of Broughton, whose enthusiasm was only surpassed by her beauty, sat on horseback beside the Cross, with a drawn sword in her hand, and her person profusely decorated with white ribbons, which signified devotion to the House of Stuart.' After Culloden, Chambers writes later, 'Mrs Murray went abroad at her husband's request, but did not remain faithful to him.' (Note the slight but significant difference between this and Robert Fitzroy Bell's account.) The rest of her story is largely a mystery.

From John Murray's own account of the post-Culloden flight across the West Highlands, we know that she was four months pregnant at the battle. After an unsuccessful attempt to secure her safe passage through the government troops, she parted from Murray and 'came in the most private manner imaginable passing in the low Country for a Soldiers wife, and induring hardships hardly to be bore by one in health, much less by a person with a big belly, till lately accustom'd to all the care and conveniences of Life.' By the end of June 1746 she was at her mother's house in Edinburgh, where she stayed three days before being moved to a succession of safe houses (including one belonging to a Mrs Cumming which was 'fixed on as a place not suspected, it being often frequented by young Gentlemen to get cured of a desease of a very different nature') while efforts were made to procure her a passage to Holland. In September she gave birth to a son, her fourth, who however died soon after. According to Murray, her poor health and the risk of discovery prevented her from going abroad, and, if his account is true, she may have rejoined him in London about the time of his release from the Tower (March or April 1747, subsequent to Lovat's execution). An incident in 1749 indicates that the Murrays were still in contact, if not together: the Reverend James Leslie, some-time chaplain to Lord Traquair, had pawned a gold repeater watch belonging to Mrs Murray, in order to raise money for Alastair Ruadh, eldest son of the chief of Glengarry, who was in exile and so destitute that he had been forced to sell his sword and shoe-buckles. Leslie had John Murray's permission but not his wife's, and she was very angry at the disposal of her property. Murray apparently reconciled her to the loss, but thereafter she is absent from the historical record. Murray, according to Chambers, 'dragged out a wretched life upon a pension of £200 a year', and died in 1777 at Cheshunt, Hertfordshire, possibly insane. Of his wife, the historian Andrew Lang wrote, 'when Mrs Murray left her intolerable lord is not exactly known, nor is anything certain about her later fortunes'.

Buchan, then, was able to mythologise her for the purposes of his fiction, despite his misgivings about her as 'a very bad lot'. As Professor David Daniell has commented, he gave her a romantic ferocity quite unlike anything in Buchan's previous female characters, Marjory Veitch in *John Burnet of Barns* or the 'pretty misses of the modern short stories in *Grey Weather*.' Francis may not be able to draw his sword on a woman, but in his early career he was not above striking an Edinburgh whore with his open hand, sending her staggering with a blow that 'comforted his soul'. Yet it is he who is assaulted by the woman he comes to worship, Mrs Murray, when she discovers him to be, as she believes, no more than a treacherous servant. Here a whole range of emotions, charged with a sexual current that will run between the two throughout the novel, is on display:

> . . . she struck Francis full in the face with her lash.
>   . . . Francis stood immovable, his mind crushed and writhing, his cheeks flaming with disgrace. This bright creature before him had tumbled his palace of cards about his ears. He felt with acid bitterness the full ignomy, the childish, servile shame of his position. The charm of her young beauty drove him frantic; her whole mien, as of a world unknown to him and eternally beyond his reach, mocked him to despair . . . He stood with bowed head, not daring to meet her arrogant eyes, careless of the lash which curled round his cheek and scarred his brow.

> Marvellous the power of that slender arm! He felt the
> blood trickle over his eyes and half blind him, but he
> scarce had a thought of pain.

This is the start, not of a love affair (although later it threatens to become one), but of a love-hate relationship. Something in him resists the urge to retaliate and overpower her, and he realises that his renunciation of virtue is a feeble delusion: he can no more turn off the path of virtue than he can consciously follow it. 'Dimly he saw that her gaze was fixed on his bleeding forehead, and in her look he seemed to see a gleam of pity and at her mouth a quiver of regret. Then with crazy speed he ran blindly to the open moor.'

It is a key moment: we are at the mercy of feelings and obligations quite beyond our control, Buchan seems to be saying, and are swept along by powers that surge both within and around us. This is as true for Margaret as it is for Francis; for John Murray, Lovat and all. All our youthful struggles, Buchan concludes (at twenty-two!), are just the 'brave flickerings of life' before 'the ageless quiet of our destiny'. Virtue, if it befalls us, may not be lovely to gaze upon, like Margaret Murray, but, like the portrait of Francis Birkenshaw as provost of Dysart, be 'grey-haired, hard-faced . . . with cold unfriendly-looking eyes'. The moral compass swings wildly for a while, then settles with resignation to its true bearing and thereafter – so we are told – never again wavers. Perhaps this tells us something about the personality and values, not of Francis Birkenshaw, but of John Buchan himself. In any case, it is an austere, compelling ending, with its own strange beauty.

James Robertson

To
Duncan Grant Warrand

To you, the well-read historian, there is little need to say that every event in this tale is not recorded for gospel. It is the story of the bleak side of the 'Forty-five, of goodness without wisdom, of wisdom first cousin to vice, of those who, like a certain lord, had no virtue but an undeniable greatness. You will ask my authority for Francis' mission to Lovat – or the singular conduct of Mr John Murray. You will inquire how the final execution came six months too soon, and you will ransack Broughton's 'Journal' in vain to find my veracious narrative of the doings of his beautiful wife. Such little matters are the chronicler's licence. But some excuse is needed for the introduction of your kinsman, the Lord President, and the ragged picture of so rare a character. My apology must be that on my canvas there was no room for full-length portraits of statesmanship and honesty.

Such as it is, I dedicate to you this chronicle of moorland wars, for the sake of an 'auld Highland story', which neither of us would wish to see forgotten.

JB
June 1899

Contents

'E'en so, swimmingly appears,
Through one's after supper musings,
Some lost lady of old years
With her beauteous vain endeavour
And goodness unrepaid as ever.'
                                    Browning

BOOK I

The Birkenshaws of that Ilk and their Fortunes

When Gideon Birkenshaw – of Birkenshaw Tower in the Forest and the lands of Markit beneath the brow of Cheviot – was summoned by death to his account, he left all to his eldest son and turned the other penniless upon the world. Robert, the heir, stepped unthinking into the dead man's shoes, and set himself to the family task of amassing gear. He was a man already grim and ageing at thirty, with the stoop of an inquisitor and deep eyes to search out the intents of the heart. Of old the house had been insignificant raiders, adding field to field and herd to herd by a method which it seemed scarce fair to call plunder, so staidly was it pursued. No minstrel sang their deeds, no tale of them was told at nightfall in the village, but in all decency and hardness they went like oxen to their resting places. They cared naught for politics, but every now and again the stock bred a religious enthusiast. A Birkenshaw had served with the Lords of the Congregation, and another had spoken his testimony in the face of the Grassmarket and a thousand people, and swung off valiantly into eternity. The watchword of all was decency and order, and as peace settled upon the land they had left off their old huntings and harryings and fallen to money-making with the heartiest goodwill. And they prospered deservedly. While the old poor Tweedies, Horsebrocks, and Burnets, whose names were in a hundred songs and tales, who had fought with quix- otic gallantry always on the losing side, and spent their substance as gaily as they had won it, sank into poverty and decline, the crabbed root of the Birkenshaws budded and put forth shoots. With anxious eyes and prayerful lips they held on their wonted path, delighting in the minutes of bargaining and religious observance, yet full of pride of house and brave with the stubborn valour of the unimaginative.

It was indeed their pride of race, their inherited spirit, and their greater wealth which alone marked them off from the burly farmers of the countryside. To see them at kirk or market, their clothes were as coarse, their talk as rude, and their companions the same as their neighbours of the sheep-farms. But all knew and owned the distinction. Somewhere in the heavy brow and chin of a Birkenshaw there lurked passion and that ferocity which can always awe the born retainer. The flashes were scarce, but they were long remembered. When a son of the house broke the jaw of Chasehope for venturing to sell him a useless collie bitch, the countryside agreed that the man but got his deserts for seeking to overreach a Birkenshaw beyond the unwritten rules of dealing. And darker stories were told – of men maimed and slain in change-houses, even, it was whispered, at the door of the House of God, for chancing in their folly upon the family madness.

They married women like themselves, hard, prudent, and close-lipped; seeking often far and wide for such a wife and never varying from their choice. Such marriages were seldom fruitful but never barren; one or two sons were always left to hand on the name and the inheritance. No man had yet been found of sufficient courage to mate with a daughter of the house, and so it fell out that those gaunt women, strong and tall as the men, stayed in the Birkenshaw Tower till their brothers' marriage, and then flitted to the lonely dwelling of Markit, where there always waited some brother or uncle in need of a housekeeper. Such an order in life brought its reward. There were no weaklings to spoil the family credit, and like a stripped unlovely pine the stock survived, abiding solitary on its hilltop and revelling in storms.

But in their lives they paid assiduous court to a certain kind of virtue. In the old riding days the house had robbed and harried, as it were, under protest; and now, being fallen on settled times, they cultivated honesty with the greatest diligence.

A Birkenshaw's word was as good as his oath, and his oath as his bond, and woe befall the man who doubted either. The milk of human kindness was confined with them to family channels and embittered with the grudging which comes of obedience to the letter. By the canon of the Word of God they were men of a singular uprightness, but it was a righteousness which took the colour of the family traits. They set diligence, honour, and a freedom from gross vices on the one hand, and passion, relentless severity, and little love for their neighbours on the other, and, finding the result to be a species of pride, labelled it an excellence. Withal, their penuriousness made their lives frugal and their toils gave them health, so that, a race of strong men, they ran their imperious course, feared in their faults and hated in their virtues.

The pastimes of their class were little thought of. It was long since one of the name had been seen with the deerhounds or playing a salmon in the floods of Tweed. Long days of riding over their broad lands were varied with noisy mornings in the clatter of a marketplace or evenings filled with the sleep of well-fed lassitude. But when they came among their fellows it was with something of a presence – the air of masters who cared little for the quibblings of superiority but were ready if occasion came to prove it by deed. Hence came the owercomes of 'A Birkenshaw's glower', and '"Gang out o' my gate," quo' auld Birkenshaw,' with which the conversation of the valley was garnished.

In such manner did life pass by in the grey stone dwelling which crowned the Yarrow braes, with Yarrow crooning in the nooks below. It was but yesterday I passed the place, which no lapse of years can change. The vale of long green hills which falls eastward from the lochs is treeless and desert for miles, with a wan stream sweeping 'neath barren hill-shoulders and the grey-green bent lending melancholy to all. But of a sudden it changes to a defile; the hills huddle together till the waters can scarce find passage; and a forest of wild-wood chokes the gorge. Brown heather and green hazels crest every scarred rock and fringe the foot of Birkenshaw Tower, which looks steeply

down on its woodland valley. Soft meadow-grass is shaded by a
tangle of ashes, and in every dell the burn's trickle slips through
a wild flower garden; while in broad pools and shining stretches
Yarrow goes singing her ageless song for evermore.

Of the two sons born to Gideon Birkenshaw in the house on
the hill, the elder was even as his father, a man of few words and
hard deeds, ungenial, honest, and with all his qualities grounded
on that rock of devilment which lay deep in the temper of his
house. His person was even as his nature, and it was not hard
to see in the spare and sinewy figure of the son the immature
presentment of the father. But the younger, Francis, was like a
changeling in the place. From his birth he had none of the ways
of the rest; his very form was like a caricature of the family
traits, and whatever was their strength was in him perverted to
weakness. He had the Birkenshaw high cheekbones, the fleshy
chin and the sunken eyes, but all were set carelessly together, as
if by nature in a moment of sport. He had his father's long
limbs and broad back, but in him the former were feeble and
knoitering, the latter bent in an aimless stoop. In character the
parody was the more exaggerated. Shrewdness became a
debased cunning which did not halt at a fraud; energy, mere
restlessness; and persistence, stupidity. Also the mastery over
the bodily appetites which marked the kin was wholly absent in
him, and early in life he took to brandy drinking and tavern
loafing. Every fold has its black sheep and every house its weak-
ling, but to the proud family whence he sprung Francis was
something more than a ne'er-do-weel. He was a lasting disgrace,
always at the doors, staring in their faces at kirk and market. It
is the curse of such a kin that a man who shows somewhat
weaker than the rest marches straight to the devil without a
chance of redemption, and the house of Birkenshaw with drawn
lips and averted eyes suffered the prodigal to go his way.

But in the trivial Mr Francis there remained some shreds
and rags of quality unperceived by his kinsfolk. He alone in
the whole history of his race possessed a tincture of the
humanities, picked up in a ragged way but worthy of note. He

had something of a poetic soul and saw wonders in hill and water which were not for the busy men of affairs who rode their horses over the countryside solely that they might reach an end. He was humane in little matters, and no dumb creature suffered ill usage at his hands. Even in his vices he preserved some tatters of kindliness which endeared him to the folk with whom he consorted. In a dim, confused way he strove to guide his shambling life in the way of mercy, and in his stumbling made helpless efforts to rise.

It was clear to all that such a state of matters could not long continue, and the mind of the countryside waited for a crisis. It arrived at length and in the expected way. The blacksmith of Birkenshaw was one Reuben Gowanlock, a drunken, ill-conditioned fellow, with a set hatred of the family in the Tower and a marvellous power of quarrelling. His daughter Marion, a handsome girl of twenty, fell much in the way of Mr Francis in his village sojournings, and an intimacy sprang up between them which endured all through the spring and summer of a year. No record exists of its nature, but it is certain that the couple took long walks in the sunset vale, during which Francis would charm her ears with his flowery rhapsodic talk and her vanity with his presence. In the winter a child was born, and in the eyes of all the laird's son stood confessed as the father. The blacksmith cursed deep and swore vengeance; poor Marion dared not show herself abroad; and things looked black enough for both. But worse was still to follow, for the place was startled one morn by the news that Francis had married the girl in all good faith. Here was food for gossip and speculation, and it was the common verdict that the man had made reparation in terror of Reuben's menaces. Yet it is certain that nothing was less in Francis' mind. Whatever grave lack he had there was no stint in his share of the family courage. His motive for the deed was an indistinct sense of honour, a certain ill-defined compassionateness of heart, which he scarcely realized and would not have sought to defend.

For the twain the end came sharp and cruel. There was long speech in the place of the interview between Francis and his father, and stray fragments of what passed were spread abroad.

The wretched creature with his farcical handsomeness stood shivering before the terrible old man, who represented the essence of a long line which knew no mercy. Every inch of his face was browned and wrinkled with sun and wind; his eye glanced steely as an October sun; and his figure was alive with vigour and wrath. He had been absent on a visit to Markit when the events occurred, and all was over ere he returned. So in riding-boots and greatcoat he sat at the table's end with a hunting crop before him. He heard the village explanation of his son's folly and he was not slow to believe it. His sentences came out with a dry rasp and with an ominous accompaniment of lowering brows, 'I will not speak of the crime against God's law as written in His book, for that is a matter between you and your saul.' Indeed, it was said that others of the Birkenshaws had erred in like manner, and in any case it was not a sin which involved any surcease of pride. 'But of one thing I will speak,' he went on, 'and that is of your offence against the bluid of the man that begat ye and the house that gives ye your name. Ye have mairrit a tinkler lass, ye splaittering body, because ye were feared at her faither's mauvering. By God, there was never yet ane o' your race wi' sic a taid's hert.'

The wretched son made no attempt at a defence which he would have scarcely told to himself. He shuffled with ineffectual feeling, a prey to sentiment and inward tears.

'But "my son" did I say?' the other went on. 'Na, na, ye are nae son o' mine. Gang to the midden ye've been pikin' on and let a cleanly honest house be quit o' ye. Gang off, the pair o' ye, and breed up bairns to rin for porters and serve in byres. By the Lord Almichty I disown ye, and I wis nae mair than to see ye in the kennel ye've made for yoursel'. Gang out o' my sicht, ye thing o' strae.'

Francis went out of the room with an indistinct pain of heart, for he was no more than sober from his morning cups. Yet the grating tones had scarcely ceased, the door was scarcely closed, ere the old man laid his head on his hands and suffered in dry-eyed misery the pangs of pride wounded through affection.

Of the exact movements of Mr Francis after that hour there remains no adequate tale. He could not bide in the house, nor did his remnants of pride suffer him to remain in the village. With such small belongings as were his he took himself and his wife to Edinburgh, and set up dwelling in a dingy room in the Monk's Vennel. How he lived no man could tell, but it seems likely that when all his gear had gone for brandy this scion of a reputable house did odd jobs for whoever was willing to hire him, from copying a bill to carrying a bundle. One thing is certain, that his course, whatever it was, soon drew to an end. His body was never strong, and his impressionable and capricious temper of mind was not far removed from craziness. Poverty and dram-drinking so wrought upon him that soon he was little better than an enfeebled idiot, sitting melancholy on tavern benches and feeding the fire of life on crude spirits. Two more children – daughters – were born to him, and some five years after his departure from home Mr Francis Birkenshaw had become a mere wreck of his former wreckage, a parody of a parody. Six months later a fever took him, and kindly Death stepped in with his snuffer and turned the guttering candle into blackness.

Hitherto we have not spoken of Mistress Marion Birkenshaw, who adorned the dim house in the Monk's Vennel. Her beauty, at first considerable, had grown with the years to heaviness, and naught remained but singular black eyebrows. Her nature was not extraordinary, but rejoiced in the niceties of gossip and the refinements of housekeeping. Her early behaviour was the sudden blossoming of romance in an orderly mind, and with the advancing months she returned to the placid level of the common. Had she married decently and dwelt in her native village she would have been a matron without reproach, a mistress of gossip and old-wives' tales, glorying in little hospitalities and petty hatreds. As it was, she ruled her household with a bustling hand, and found neighbours in a desert of strangers. The clack of her tongue sounded all day about the doors, or was sunk in the afternoon to a contented sing-song when Mistress Gilfillan dropped in to sew with her and tell her woes.

Even in so hard a place she attained to some measure of happiness, and ordered sprawling children and feckless husband with a pride in the very toil. Loud-tongued, noisy, coarse as sackcloth, a wallower in the juicily sentimental, she yet had something of the spirit of a general, and marshalled her ragged forces in decent array.

On the death of Mr Francis her action took a characteristic path. For, meeting Robert, now master of the broad lands of Birkenshaw, in the High Street one chill February morn, she forthwith detailed to him his brother's debts, and with the abandon of her class glided from becoming tears into the necessary question of maintenance. The Laird's feelings at the moment would be hard to tell. The thought that one of his house should have sunk so low that his widow had to beg her bread, stung him like a lash. He lost for the moment his habitual reserve. With a mumbled 'Tak it, wumman, tak it; there'll be mair to follow,' he thrust some gold into her hand; and thenceforth came quarterly payments from Birkenshaw with a bare word of communication. Marion took them gladly, for she had no other choice, and on such means she reared her children to grown age.

One incident in her character remains which is eloquent in its strangeness. From the day of her departure she held no communication with her folk at the smithy, manifesting no interest in their doings and shunning even the mention of their names. Deep in her soul was a well of sentiment. She had mated with a Birkenshaw, and some peace-offering was due to the fetich of the family pride. A sense of an honour paid to her hung ever on her conscience; it made her look with respect on her own children as something higher than herself; and it forced her to the severance of natural ties. It is doubtful, indeed, whether they were ever tightly knit, for the drunken father had little kindness for any. But, such as they were, they were gladly renounced, and with something not far from heroism this foolish woman took loneliness for her portion, a solitude brightened with the halo of a great connection.

TWO

How Mr Francis Birkenshaw
Departed his Native City

The child Francis grew up to manhood with precipitancy, for in that house life was not suited for a lengthy play-day. At five he had been as ugly as sin in face, though well-grown and straight in body. His father's hard features and ruddy skin were joined to Marion's sloe-black eyes and hair, and such a conjunction is not fair in childhood. So peculiarly sinister an appearance would have made him the butt of his coevals, had he not possessed a hot temper and an uncommonly hard fist. From his sixth year battles were of daily occurrence, and it was rarely that the weekend found him with his face unmarked. But inch by inch, wound by wound, he fought his way to fame, till the mere sight of his black countenance was more than enough to hush the wrangling of the others and incline their ears to his words.

But with those days we have little to do, and it is at the maturity of eighteen that we would take up the tale of his life. His sisters, Jean and Lisbeth, were now grown to high-coloured, loud-spoken girls, who shared their mother's likings and their mother's comeliness. The Birkenshaw payments made comfort possible, and the house was conducted in a pleasant stir, with gossips sitting at all hours and the sharp tones of the housewife guarding its cleanliness and order. The two lasses were the blacksmith's true grandchildren, and in no way different from a thousand such maids in the city. They loved to dress in their best of a Sabbath and walk in decent procession to the Cross Kirk, where the ministrations of Mr Linklater were sugared with the attentions of the young apprentices. They were notable

cooks and 'wrought all day to their mother's bidding with a
cheery bustle. In a word, they were of their mother's pattern –
honest, fresh-coloured, hearty, and forthcoming to all.

Had it not been for their brother's presence, the household in
the Monk's Vennel might have been an abode of prosperous
peace. But Francis was a puzzle to most folk and a grief to his
mother such as her foolish loose-lived husband had never been.
The years brought him height and strength and a handsome
face. It would have been hard to find in all the town a nobler
figure of a youth, when anger did not distort the features. From
some unknown forebear he derived an air of uncommon
masterfulness, and a carriage which might have vied with that
of the greatest buck of the day, my Lord Craigforth himself. His
temper was like his body, fierce and strong, and hot as a red fire,
so that no man could anger him with safety. In happier conditions he might have followed the paths of virtue, for there
seemed nothing ignoble in that brow and eye. But in the kitchen
of his home, among the clatter of neighbour tongues and
women's gossip, in the presence of his mother and sisters
and the rotund housewives who called them friends, he was
woefully out of place.

In his childhood he had cared little for the thing, for the street
was his home at most hours; but as he grew to age the whole life
oppressed him with deep disgust. To him alone had fallen a
share of the Birkenshaw temper, and he revolted from this
unctuous existence. For his kin he had fits of tenderness, but at
his age no feeling is so weak as domestic love. The result was
not hard to foresee. With such share as he had of the family
income he took to his own pleasures, and the house saw him
not save at meal-times and the late night.

Who shall tell of the glorious Edinburgh of that day in all its
colour and splendour and dirt? The eighteenth century was yet
young, the second George was but new on the throne, and in the
northern city life flowed freely and hotly in a muddy, turbulent
stream. The drums of war were still in men's memories, and
soldiers from the Castle thronged the street. In the narrow alleys

which wound like snakes among the high, dark houses there lurked filth and disease which have long since gone from the land. Ragged Highland lairds and broken gillies, fine periwigged gentlemen, ministers many with their sombre black, fine ladies and country wives, honest shepherds in homespun from the South, half the gentry of the land, as well as the staid merchant or the wandering southerner, were jostled on the narrow causeway by French agents and priests in hiding, or fell a prey at dark corners to the lurking cutpurse. Roaring east winds disturbed the trials in the Parliament House, where half a dozen learned judges administered the law, ere hurrying back to dinner and their unfinished treatises on Taste and the Sublime. And the same wind caught at the throats of half-starved loyalists shivering in entries, and praying and plotting for that day when the King should come back to his own. Every now and again the streets were in an uproar over some straggling news of a fresh landing, and the good citizens listened to the bugles on the Castle rock with a feeling of confirmed security. It was the day of riot and bright colour, of fine dresses and rags, of honest poverty and the blackguard shuffling in the same kennel – a day when no man knew his own mind or his neighbours', and the King's peace was more brittle than the King desired.

But above all it was the heyday of taverns, great houses of festivity, where beside leaping fires a motley crew dined and grew drunk in all good fellowship. The age must be thick with alarums and perils of war to produce the fine flower of tavern life. It is when a man's mind is hot with wild news or the expectation of its reception that he leaves his ingle and seeks the steaming hearth and the talk of neighbours. And who can tell of the possibilities which lie in such an evening, of a door flung open and a stranger coming full of unheard-of tales? The inn-lounger is as surely a glutton for the romantic as the adventurer upon the sea.

To such homes of the soul went Francis with more zeal than discretion. There, and not in the female atmosphere of the Monk's Vennel, he found the things in which his heart delighted.

The talk of men in its freedom and brutality was his delight, and in the motley concourse of folk he had matter for a living interest. A strain of inherited vice made the darker side of it soon cease to appal him, and in time he passed from the place of a spectator to that of a partaker in many carousals, a sworn friend to half the riff-raff in the city, the ally of loose women and causeway sots.

Yet in this springtide of wild oats there was none of the sower's zest. He was much of an amateur in vice, restrained from excess by many bonds of memory, convention, and human kindliness. His course was the recoil from the paths of fireside virtue, the outcome of something uncommon and heroical in a nature run to seed. At moments a sense of the folly of it all oppressed him, but the fatal rhetoric of a boy's thoughts put the graver reflection to flight. He would regain his self-respect by fancying himself a man of the world, living with a hand close on the springs of life, one who in all his folly was something beyond his allies. And in consequence he sank but rarely into brutish drunkenness – a sin (for the confusion of all doctrines of heredity) which had little hold upon him – and even from such lapses recovered himself with a certain alertness of spirit. Yet this was but the immaturity of his character, a thing to pass away with years, and in a little Francis might have looked to grow to a blackguard of some quality.

To his mother his life was a source of uncomprehending grief. Her efforts of kindness were now repelled and now met halfway with an inconsistency which confounded all her notions. When her son swaggered home in the small hours, or when Mistress Leithen of the Candle Row retailed strange stories of his evil-doing, the unhappy woman was less pained than mystified. Maternal affection, which for the glorifying of poor humanity is strongest in the coarsely sentimental, bade her sorrow, when all the rest of her nature bade her only wonder. So with a patience and a denseness too deep for words, she persisted in her tenderness, bore his lordly humours, and revolted his soul with a thousand nauseous vulgarities, since to the rake the only intolerable coarseness is the respectably plebeian.

Now it chanced that Fate took it upon her to order events for the saving of Francis' soul. About his eighteenth year he had entered a writer's office in the city, for no other cause than to give himself some name whereby to describe his life. An odd strain of worldly prudence kept him from neglecting his duties to dismissal point, and in a sort of careful idleness he copied deeds, visited ground for seisin, and collected rents in and out of the town. He had no ill-will to the work, provided it did not bear too hardly upon his time. But meanwhile in the burgh of Dysart, which sits perched on the steep shore of Fife, there lived a Mr Gregor Shillinglaw, who as the one lawyer in the place had a good livelihood and a busy life. He was growing old, and in the natural course bethought him of a successor. His head clerk, John Henryson, was able and willing for the place, but Mr Shillinglaw belonged to a school of men who have less respect for long services than for family ties. Once on a time a Birkenshaw had married a distant cousin of his, and the two names had a kinship in his memory. So it fell out, being in Edinburgh at the office of Trumbull and Gleed, who were Francis' masters, he saw the lad, heard his name, and was affected with a sudden kindness.

He asked after his business merits. Good, admirable, said Mr Trumbull, with a smile. And his character? Oh, well, some folk are young and fresh in blood, and the same rule does not hold for all, said the lawyer, amazed at his own heresy, but bound in honour to say nothing to the discredit of his house or servants. Mr Shillinglaw heard and was satisfied; the hint of gentlemanly vices only increased his friendliness for the young man; so before the week was out Francis received an offer to go to Dysart to a place which with care might bring him to an old age of opulence and respect.

To Dysart Francis went with a mixture of feelings. He had never lived elsewhere than in Edinburgh, and he was glad to make trial of a new habitat on the very edge of the sea. More, he had many deeds to his name in Edinburgh which would scarce bear the inevitable scrutiny which the days must bring. His credit, too, was low, and his debts great; so with a light heart and much hope he betook himself to the dark rooms in the little wind-worn town, where men's lips are always salt, with the air from the sea, and a roaring east wind sweeps in the narrow lanes.

The ancient town is now a very little place, unsightly with coal and dingy with stagnant traffic. But in the days of Mr Shillinglaw it was a bustling port, where skippers from Amsterdam came with strong waters and cheeses and Lord knows what and carried away beer and tallow, hides and sea coal. It boasted of a townhouse where the noisy burgesses met, and elegant piazzas where foreign merchants walked and chaffered. In the rock-hewn harbour lay at all times two score and more of schooners, and the high red-tiled houses looked down upon an eternal stir of shipping and unlading. It was a goodly place to live, for health came with the clean sea-wind and wealth with every tide.

Of Francis' doings in this place there is scant account save for the brilliant episode which marked his departure. It seems that at first he wrought well under Mr Shillinglaw's guidance, and the two would drink their claret of a night in all amity. But untoward events soon thickened in the younger's path, and, aided by his uncertain temper, he began anew his downward course. From the time when he first saw Nell Durward his doom was assured, and thereafter his master might grieve or storm but Francis remained untouched. Nell was the provost's daughter, tall and comely, with bright cheeks and saucy black eyes which captured his roving thoughts. Thenceforth he was her slave, running at her every beck and nod, till her father, with some inkling of how matters stood, resolved to put an end to his daughter's coquetry, and plainly told the eager lover that Nell was already betrothed to a bailie of the town, one Gow by name, and would shortly be his wife.

Francis flung himself out of the house, and from that hour till after the celebration of the wedding drank more deeply than he had ever done before, and bade Mr Shillinglaw and his business to go to the devil whence they had come. For three weeks he was the byword of the place; then, when all was over, he returned to his right mind and relapsed into decency with some apology for his absence.

But Fate had still further tricks to play on him. It chanced that a yearly dinner was held in the Bunch of Grapes in memory of some former benefactor of the town, and thereafter dancing went on till morning in the roomy upper chamber, where faded silk hangings and a frowning portrait proclaimed antiquity. Hither went Francis in a sober mood, and after the meal drank his toddy with the fathers of the burgh as befitted a grave notary. But after he had his fill of their company and had grown hot with the fumes of spirits, he mounted the stair, and sitting by the fiddlers surveyed the gay scene. Suddenly to the assembly there entered Bailie Gow, with the aforetime Nell Durward blushing on his arm. The devil of boastfulness, born of early and deep potations, drove the husband in the direction of his rival. He gaped before him, and then with many abusive words delivered him a moral homily. The blood of Francis, hot at the best, was roused to madness by the man's conduct and the thought of his own unrewarded love. 'Let go his arm, my dear,' he said quietly to the girl, and struck the portly bailie clean on the jaw so that he dropped like a felled ox.

Now Mr Gow was a great man in the town, and at the sight a party, with the landlord, one Derrick, at their head, made to lay hands on his assailant. But Francis was strong and young, and with a bench he cleared a space around him and fought his way to the door. His head was in a muddle, and his one thought was to reach the street. But at the stair-top the landlord confronted him, and with a cudgel struck him smartly on the face. The blow roused madness to action. With a sudden crazy resolution Francis drew a knife and stabbed the man in the side, and then breaking through the crowd on the steps reached the open and ran straight for the distant woods.

The remainder of the incident goes with still greater spirit. For three days Francis lay hid among the brackens with the terror of murder on his soul. But none came to seek him, and with the hours his confidence grew, till he summoned his courage and sallied out at the darkening of the fourth day. With infinite labour he avoided observation and entered the narrow wynds. Now came his chief toil. He must learn of the landlord's fate to ease his mind and determine his plans. So in much trepidation he betook himself to the only haven he could think of, the house of one Berritch, a man of rumoured wealth but no reputation, a former ally of his own in tavern-drinking, and esteemed a trafficker in the contraband.

Thither he crept, and won immediate admittance. He heard with relief that his enemy was all but recovered, that the wound had been a mere scratch, and that his name was free at least from such a stain. But otherwise, Mr Berritch admonished him, things looked black indeed. Mr Shillinglaw had repudiated him, and the respectability of the place had made their faces flint against him. It was currently believed that he had returned to Edinburgh.

In such a state of affairs Francis was ripe for an offer, and Mr Berritch did not fail him. He himself would undertake to bring him to France in one of his boats, and set him down where there was a chance and room for likely young lads unburdened with a conscience. He could not remain in Dysart, and the city was but a halting place on the road to beggary. That night a lugger would sail from Wemyss rocks in which he was welcome to a passage.

The conclusion of the episode was yet more varied; for when all had won to the starting-point, word was brought that the Burntisland gaugers had got tidings about Mr Berritch and his occupation, which would lead them that night to pay a visit to his dwelling. The unfortunate man bowed to fate in a transport of cursing, and set his face to the boat and the sea; but in the nick of time he had mind of moneys left in the house, which he would little like to see in the hands of the law. He was at his wits' end, when Francis, with the uneasy generosity of one in debt, offered to go to fetch them. Accordingly he set out and made his way through the dark and filthy east streets of Dysart, not without some qualms of anxiety. But at the High Street corner he met a man in an advanced stage of drunkenness, stumbling over ash-buckets and suffering from the narrowness of the path. A glance convinced him that it was none other than Bailie Gow, returning from some burgh dinner, and flown with wine and talk. A plan grew in Francis' mind which made him shake with mirth. Slipping his arm through the bailie's he led him to Mr Berritch's house and set him in Mr Berritch's chair, with Mr Berritch's spare wig on his head and a tumbler of rum at his elbow. Then he secured the gold, and slipped outside the window to wait the result. His patience was little tried, for soon there came the tramp of men down the street, a knocking at the door, a forced entrance, and a swoop upon their prisoner. He heard them read the paper of identification, and give a one-voiced consent to every detail. Then with aching sides and smarting eyes he watched them lift the innocent upon their shoulders; and when their tread died away he betook himself to the cutter in huge delight at his boyish humour.

With this bravado begins the history of the deeds of Mr Francis Birkenshaw, which he did in the years of our Lord seventeen hundred and forty-five and seventeen hundred and forty-six in the reign of George the Second, King of England. In such a fine fervour of conceit and daring he launched out upon his course. The events of the past weeks seemed like an ancient tale from which he was separated by years of maturity. In a night he had outgrown any vain schemes for a reputable life of citizenship. Now he was free to go whither he pleased, and carve his fortune in the manner best suiting him without restraint of prejudice. As the vessel rode on the waters and the wind sang in the sheets, his heart was strengthened with pleasing self-praise, not without a hint of mirth at the comedy of life.

But for all great designs money was needful, and Mr Berritch himself was the first to mention it. Now the secret of the Birkenshaw payments had always been kept hid from Francis, and he thought that the family substance came from some fortune of his father's. There must be a portion remaining to him, he thought, and on this he set his hope. So it was settled that the lugger should lie well into the Lothian coast during the day, and in the evening he should be put ashore to seek his own.

The plan was carried out to the letter, and at eight the next night Francis was knocking at the door of his mother's house. From within came the noise of tongues and women's laughter, and the cheerful clatter of dishes which marks the close of a meal. His mother opened to him, wiping her mouth with her apron in a way she had, and smirking over her shoulder. At the sight of him she started, and he entered unbidden. The place bore all the marks of comfort, and in the firelight he saw two women of the neighbourhood, old gossips of his sisters and mother. His entrance hushed their talk, and sidelong looks and a half-giggle succeeded. Somehow the sight roused his gorge unspeakably. He, with his mind intent upon high adventure, with the smell of the salt sea and the fierce talk of men still in his memory, loathed this glozing prosperity, these well-fed women, and the whole pettiness of life. He took his mother aside and demanded the money which was his portion. She, good soul, did not tell him the truth, but wrapping herself up in her rags of pride, went to a drawer and gave him a meagre bag of gold. It was the latest payment, and its loss meant straitened living for months. But he knew nothing of this, thought it but his share, and grumbled at its smallness. With the irony which riots in life, at that moment he was pluming himself upon superiority to such narrow souls, when all the while pride in one was making a sacrifice of which he knew nothing. His remnants of filial love made him take a kindly farewell of his mother; and then, with nose in the air and a weathercock of a brain, he shook off the dust of the domestic, and went out to the open world.

With the doorway of his former home, he passed from vice frowned upon and barely loved to vice gilded and set upon a pedestal. A sense of high exhilaration grew upon him. He would follow his own desires, with the aid of a strong hand and a courageous heart. In his then frame of mind the only baseness seemed to lie in settling upon his lees in the warm air of the reputable. A hard conscience and a ready hand were a man's truest honour, and with this facile catchword he went whistling into a new life.

But at the moment something from the past came to greet him. As he passed a tavern door a girl with the face and attire of the outcast hailed him boisterously and made to link her arm with his. He knew her well for one of his aforetime comrades. Her face was pinched, and the night wind was blowing through her thin dress. But from Francis she got no kindness. His heart at the time was too steeled on his own path for old regrets. With a curse he struck her harshly with his open hand, and watched her stagger back to the causeway. The blow comforted his soul. It was the seal upon his new course, the rubicon which at length he had crossed; and when he came to Musselburgh sands and the lugger, it was with an increased resolution in his fool's heart.

THREE

Forth and Tweed

The wind was already shaking in the sails when he clambered aboard, and the windlass groaned with the lifting anchor. Mr Berritch cried a cheery greeting from the bow, as Francis, heavy with sleep, tumbled down below to bed. The moon was up, the night airs were fine, and in a little the lugger was heading by the south end of Inchkeith for the swell of the North Ocean.

At dawn Francis was up and sniffing the salt air over the bulwarks. A landsman born, he had little acquaintance with the going down to the sea in ships, and the easy movement and the brisk purpose of the lugger delighted his heart. He was still in the first heat of adventure; the white planking, the cordage, the tarry smell were all earnests of something new; and with the vanishing smoke and spires he beheld the end of a life crimped and hampered. He felt extraordinary vigour of body and a certain haphazard quality of mind which added breadth to his freedom. But at the last sight of the Pentlands' back, sentiment woke for one brief moment ere she shook her wings and fled.

He turned from his meditation to find Mr Berritch at his elbow with a smile and a good morning. Seen in the first light his face had an ugly look about the eyes and ponderous jaw, a shadow in the lines of his mouth. With him came another, whose face Francis had not seen before – a lean youth with bleak eyes, a hanging chin, and a smirk always on the verge of his lips.

'Ye came well off frae your venture, Francie,' said Mr Berritch. 'I have to present to ye Mr Peter Stark, a young gentleman out o' Dumbarton, bound on the same errand to France as yoursel'. Starkie, this is Mr Birkenshaw I telled ye o'.'

The two bowed awkwardly, and the elder man went off and left them. Francis got little comfort from the sight of the gawky boy before him. If this were a type of the gentleman-adventurer, then it would have suited better with his tastes to have chosen another trade. As for Mr Stark, he assumed an air of wonderful shrewdness, which raw youth at all times believes to be the mark of the man of affairs.

'What's garred ye take the road, Mr Birkenshaw?' said he, with the drawling accent of the West.

The other looked him up and down with rudeness and leisure, scanning every detail of his rustic clothes, his ill-tied hair, and the piteous aping of the fine gentleman in his carriage. This was no better than the tavern sots in Edinburgh with whom he had brawled a year before.

'What if I do not care to make my business public on every shipboard, sir?' he said with chill insolence. 'Do you think I should go about making proclamation of my past?'

The boy looked aggrieved and taken back. 'But between men of honour,' he said sullenly.

Francis laughed the laugh of the man to whom all old burdens are now but the merest names. 'Honour!' he said, with a sense of diplomacy in the assumption of a part, 'honour is not a luxury for you or me, my friend. We're running atween the jaws o' government warships, and whatever we may have done it's unlikely that there'll be much talk o' fair trial for suspects. Every man is his neighbour's enemy till he has put his breast before him to the bullet. Then there may be friendship. But what talk is this of honour, sir, atween two chance acquaintances?' And he stood, darkly suspicious, in a fervour of self-admiration.

The other bent low in respect for this new revelation of spirit. He felt a tingle of shame for his petty villainies in the presence of one whose crimes might yet be called high treason. By a mere chance Francis had fallen upon the part best suited to take his comrade's fancy. Henceforth he might act as he pleased and yet loom heroic to the reverent eyes of Mr Stark. The frank homage pleased him, and he felt a morsel of liking for this uncouth Westlander. So leaning over the rail, they spoke of their joint fortunes.

With the freshets of the wider seas Francis rose in spirits. His mind, in the Edinburgh and Dysart days, had always been panoramic, raking the future with its spyglass and finding solace in visions. He had never entered a brawl or a debauch without some glimpse of himself in the act of cutting a fine figure to cheer his fancy. For the mere approval of gossip he had cared little, but much for the verdict of a certain select imaginary coterie who kept house in his brain. Now his part was the adventurer, and he sought to play it to his satisfaction.

'They say that France is weel filled wi' Scots,' said Mr Stark. 'I hae near twae hunner guineas I took frae my faither, and I'm the lad to mak mair.' And he stuck his hat more jauntily, and whistled the stave of a song.

'Guineas for auld men,' said Francis. 'For me, I have little thought on gear, if I but get free hand and fair play. Lasses and gear fall soon to the high hand. Myself, I am for the King's court, the rightful King's, as a gentleman should. Ye'll be a Whig since ye come from the Westlands, Mr Stark?'

'Whig did you say? Na, na! I was a Whig yince when Kate Mallison was yin, and I gaed to the kirk to watch her. But noo I'll sing "Jamie come hame" wi' any braw lad that's to my mind.' And the boy grimaced and swaggered.

Something in the attitude struck the finical Francis with disgust. This Dumbarton apprentice had not the figure or speech of a King's man.

He was on the point of giving him back some rude gibe, when a thought of his new part smote upon him. He checked his tongue and held a diplomatic peace. To the true master no tool was too feeble for use, so he set to to flatter Mr Stark.

It may be guessed that the task prospered, for soon the face of the one beamed with conscious worth. Then the voice of Mr Berritch broke roughly in upon the colloquy.

'Heh, Starkie, come and gie's a lift wi' this wecht.'

The boy looked queerly at his companion and ambled off to

obey. He came back with face flushed from stooping, only to find in Francis a mood of stony disdain.

For a little he looked out to sea and bit his lips. Then he said in accents of apology: 'He askit little to tak me ower, so I maun needs help him in his bit jobs.'

'I have nothing to do with your affairs,' said his immovable comrade, 'but I would be sweered to fetch and carry for any man. And what talk is this o' money? Does he charge hire like an Alloa ferryman?'

To the bargaining mind of the other such a tone seemed uncalled for. 'Ye wadna expect him to dae't for love? I couldna dae't mysel'.'

'Then, by God, Mr Stark, ye have most of the lessons of gentility to learn.'

At this moment of time the voice of Mr Berritch was again audible. He came aft the vessel with his brow shining from toil. Now, on the high seas, he was a different man from the secret gentleman of Dysart. His tones were boisterous and full of authority, his eye commanding, and his figure trimmer. More, his jaw looked uglier, and his narrow, unkindly eyes a full half more disconcerting.

'Starkie, my lad,' he shouted, 'ye maun come and gie's a hand. And you, Mr Birkenshaw, gang to the bows, and help Tam Guthrie wi' the ropes. I'm terrible shorthanded this voyage, and I canna hae idlers.'

The hectoring note roused contradiction in Francis' blood. He bore no dear affection for Mr Berritch, and he had no mind to serve him. He scarcely even felt the debt of obligation, for had he not already risked his liberty for the captain's gold?

'Ye would not have me work like a tarry sailor, Mr Berritch?' said he.

'E'en so,' said the bold ship's captain. 'I would have ye work like a tarry sailor when ye're on my lugger.' And he looked the young man up and down with insolent eye.

Francis became for the moment magnanimous. 'If ye were to ask it as a favour, I would be the first to oblige ye, but . . .'

The other cut him short, frowning.

'Weel, weel, sir, if ye're mindit to play the fine gentleman ye can dae it and be damned to ye. But ye'll pay me twenty guineas down for your passage, when I micht hae been content wi' ten if ye had shown decent civility.'

Francis grew dusky with sudden wrath.

'I thought I had paid ye for my passage already,' said he hoarsely. 'Besides, I had a thought that there was a talk o' friendship in the matter.'

Mr Berritch laughed long and loud. 'Is't like,' he said, 'when ye winna dae a bit obleegement when I ask ye? Na, na, my man, ye'll gie me the twenty afore ye steer frae thae boards, and seein' that ye're payin' for it a' ye can take your leisure like a gentleman.'

It would be hard to tell the full irritation of his hearer's mind. To be blocked and duped thus early in his career of adventure by a knavery more complete than his own, was bitter as wormwood. A certain trust in the generous and the friendly had remained to him even in his renunciation of virtue, and now its loss seemed more vexatious than consisted with his new view of the world. He was in a maze of self-distrust and wounded sentiment, to which, as the minutes passed, was joined the more wholesome passion of anger.

For one brief second he was tempted to a curious course. He had almost paid the money demanded, posed as the wounded friend, and continued in that lofty character. But the feeling passed, and his vexation sealed his resolve to send Mr Berritch and his crew to the devil rather than yield.

'What's he taking from you?' he asked Starkie, who stood watching the result with the interest of malice.

'He's daein' it for ten,' was the answer.

'Then this is my word to you, Mr Berritch,' and Francis drew himself up. 'Ye offered to take me over for friendliness, and, though we fall out over the matter of friendship, I hold ye to your bargain. You land me in France hale and safe, or I'll ken the reason why,' and he tapped his sword-handle with rising pride.

'And this is my word to you, Mr Birkenshaw,' said the captain, his face aflame with rage. He had flung down the rope end, and stood with arms on hips and blazing eyes. 'I hae three men here wi' me, ilka ane a match for you, and I mysel' could soon gar ye pit up your bit swirdie. But I'm a man o' peace, and I likena violence. If ye dinna pay me your farin' here and now, I land ye in Berwick afore night, whaur I ken o' some who will hae meikle to say to ye aboot your misdeeds.'

The man's whole carriage had changed from the bluff bravado he had once affected to an air of cunning and respectable malice. Francis felt the hopelessness of his case, and his thoughts grew hotter. He drew his blade and was in the act of rushing upon his foe when that worthy whistled shrilly, and at the sign the three ship hands, truculent fellows all, came running to his side. Francis glanced toward Starkie and there read the folly of his action. If the Westlander had but joined him he would have forth-with attacked the quarto with good will. But his comrade clearly had no love for the sight of steel, for with a very white face and shaking legs he was striving to act the mediator.

The captain regarded his opponent grimly and calmly. As the anger ebbed from Francis' brain his reason returned and he looked on his folly with some little shame. But sufficient remained to make him obdurate. 'Take me to Berwick if it please ye,' he cried, 'but ye'll never see the glint o' my money.'

'To Berwick ye'll gang,' was the sour answer, 'and I wish ye may like it.' And without more words he went about his business.

Francis went over to the gunwale and looked out to sea. The September day was ending in a drizzle of mist and small rain. He could not see the shore, save as a dim outline; but he guessed that they must be well down the Berwick coast, seeing that they had rounded the Bass in the early morning. The threat of Mr Berritch had no special terrors for him, his misdeeds were out of the region of actual crime, and in any case Berwick was too far away for punishment. But, unless he liked to face a ship's crew and captain with the bare sword, he would be carried igno-miniously into harbour, and find himself stranded purposeless once more in his own land. And yet he would never pay the money, he reflected, as he became cognizant of his own root of pride. He had sudden yearnings towards virtue, produced by his sudden disgust at villainy in another. But above all the bitterness rose highest that he should be thus frustrated in the first glamour of his hopes.

The gallant Mr Stark came up with consolations – not without timidity. His respect for his companion had grown hugely in the last minutes, and he was disposed himself to assume something of a haughty bearing. But he got no word from the sullen figure at the bulwarks, till he had exhausted his vocabulary of condolence.

'Mr Birkenshaw,' said he, 'I hae a word to say to ye anent your ways o' getting to France. I haena your experience, but I can see wi' my ain een that this road is no the safest. If ye were to land in Berwick, it's no abune ninety mile across the country to the west. Ye could walk it in three days, and there ye'd find a boat to set ye ower for something less than this man's twenty guineas.'

Francis flamed up in wrath. 'And ye would have me carried ashore like a greeting child! No, by God, though I have to sweem for it, that man and his folk will never lay their tarry hands on me,' and he stared fiercely into the mist.

But as he looked and meditated some fragments of a plan began to grow up in his brain. It would be little to his disadvantage to cross the land and embark from the west. It would save him the intolerable humiliation of a voyage in Mr Berritch's company and another scene of wrangling at the end. Moreover, it would save him money, and somewhere in Francis, now that he was cast on himself, there lurked a trace of the old Birkenshaw providence. Again, it would keep up his reputation in the eyes of Starkie and his own self-respect; both weighty considerations for a vain man. But the matter of the landing still stuck in his throat and had all but driven him to the paths of prudence.

Then Mr Stark spoke out with resolution.

'It maitters little to me what way I gang, and I thocht o' offering ye my company. Twae men are aye better than yin, and I ken the Westland.' The offer screwed Francis' decision to the point of some crazy piece of bravado, and none the less stirred some hidden generosity.

'I have taken a great liking to ye, Mr Stark,' he replied with condescension, 'and I own I'll be glad o' your company. But there's one thing I must tell you if ye would come with me. If when we come to Berwick they offer to put hands on me and set me in their bit boat, there and then I gang overboard and sweem ashore. Are you fit for the ploy, Mr Stark?'

'Sweem,' cried the other joyfully, seeing in this a chance of bravery without peril. 'I was bred aside the sea, and I've leeved in the water since I was a bairn.'

It might have been five in the afternoon, but in the misty weather it was hard to guess the time. They were coasting near the land, for the light breeze was clear behind them, and the water lay deep under the shadow of the craggy shore. Through the haze they could discern the red face of the cliffs, thatched with green and founded on a chaos of boulders. Even there they heard the lap of water on the beach above the ceaseless hiss of rain. Gulls hung uneasily about their track, and through the damp air came the cry of sandpipers, thin and far. It was mournful weather and the heart of the soaked and angry Francis suffered momentary desolation.

But he was recalled to action by the harsh voice of Mr Berritch behind him. 'Well, my lad,' said the captain, 'are ye in a better frame o' mind? Yonder's Berwick and the mouth o' Tweed, and yonder ye gang if ye dinna dae my bidding. So if we are to continue our way thegether, I'll trouble you for your guineas, Mr Birkenshaw.'

Francis looked over the gunwale to the low shore, not three hundred yards off. A glimpse of house and wall to the left showed where the town began. To hesitate would be to end all his bravado in smoke, so he glanced with meaning at the excited Starkie and spoke up with creditable boldness –

'I told ye before, I'm thinking, Mr Berritch, that you would get no guineas of mine, and I'm no used to go back on my word.'

'Then we'll hae the boat,' said the captain. 'Geordie, get the boat oot.'

'And I have something more to say to ye, ye thief o' a Fife packman. Ye've matched me this time with your promises and smirks, but I'll win my ways without ye and pay ye for a' this and mair some day. So I'll bid ye good day, Mr Berritch, till our next meeting.'

And with this tearful defiance he was over the bulwarks, followed by the dauntless Stark, leaving the grim Mr Berritch some way between irritation and laughter. Two heads dipped on the misty waters, and a little after two mortals were wringing their clothes on the sanded beach.

FOUR

A Journey in Late Summer

The cold of the water dispersed Francis' high sentiment. He shook himself ruefully, and looked back at the dim outline of the ship. The journey had fairly tired him, and it vexed him to see Starkie, the better swimmer, as active as ever. But by the time he had wrung his clothes and shaken the salt from his hair his spirits had returned, and with the other at his heel he clambered up the bank of red earth and made for the nearest houses.

The darkening was already on the fall, and the roofs of the town shone faint over a field of corn. The plashing Mr Francis had no care to find a road, but held straight through the crops with a fine disregard of ownership. At the end they came to a low stone dyke, and beyond it a muddy road of the same unfriendly colour of soil. Thence the cobbles began and a line of little houses, stretching steeply down to what seemed a wide grey flood. For a second Francis' heart quickened with interest. This was the great river of Tweed, from whose banks came his family and his name. The sight momentarily enlivened for him the listless scene and the clammy weather.

Both were hungry and cold, and there was little cause to be finical in the matter of lodging; for to both these young adventurers thriftiness was something of a noble quality, and they sought to husband their present resources. So they went boldly to the first door in the line of houses and sought admittance.

A woman came, a tall, harsh-featured woman of forty and more, with her arms bare and her coats kilted. She stared at the intruders with incivility, and waited their question.

'Can you give us a bed for the night, mistress? We are two seafaring men who came ashore the day and are ettlin' to travel up the water to our hames. We're unco wet and famished, and will pay ye for all that ye may gie us.'

'Whatna vessel came ye aff?' said the woman, with suspicion in her eye.

'The *Kern* o' Leith,' said Francis readily.

'And whaur may your hames be?'

'In Yarrow at the Tinnies' Burnfoot,' seizing upon the only place of which he had heard the names.

'The Tinnies' Burn,' said the woman meditatively. 'There were Scotts in it in my time, but I heard they had flitted. Ye'll be some o' the new folk. Come in, and I'll see what I can dae for ye!'

And she led the ready pair into the kitchen.

The place was high and wide, with cobwebbed, smoke-grimed rafters and a searching odour of comfort. But soon the heat drew the salt fumes from the wet garments, and the place smelt like a ship's cabin. The woman sniffed and bustled angrily. Then with some brusqueness she bade them get up to the garret and put on her husband's breeks, for she would have no sailor-folk making her kitchen like the harbour end.

Dry clothes and the plain warm meal which followed restored the two to their natural cheerfulness. They sat by the fire and fell to speaking in low tones about their way overland to the west. It was an ill-timed action, for the housewife's suspicious ears caught names which she liked ill, and the whispering made her uneasy. She came over to the ingle and with arms squared broke in on the talk.

'What garred ye come ashore sae ill set-up, lads? I've seen mony sailor-men, but nane sae puirly fitted as yoursels.'

'We're juist ashore for a wee,' said Francis. 'We got the chance o' winnin' hame and we took it. Twae days will bring us to Yarrow, twae days back, and by that time the *Kern* 'ill be lying loadin' in the harbour. It wasna an errand to tak ony plenishing wi' us.'

The woman laughed sardonically. 'What bit o' the harbour did ye lie in?' said she.

Francis was at a loss, and cast about warily for an answer.

'I've never been here but the yince,' said he, 'so I canna just tell ye richt. But we cam maybe a hundred yairds up the river and syne cast anchor by the wall.'

Again the woman laughed. 'And how did ye win up the river? Did ye a' get oot and shove the boat wi' your shouthers?'

'Are you daft, wife?' said the dumbfoundered Mr Stark.

'No, my lad,' said she; 'but ye're the daft anes to come to me wi' a story like that. The river the noo is no three feet deep a' ower wi' sands and the shift o' the tide-bar. Ye're nae sailors. I warrant ye dinna ken a boom frae a cuddie's tail, and yet ye come here wi' your talk o' sailors. Na, I'll tell ye what ye are. Ye're Hielandmen or French, I'll no say which, but ye're ower here on nae guid errand. Ye cam frae a ship; but it was in a boat under the Tranen rocks. Oot o' my house ye gang, and ye may bless the Lord I dinna rin ye to the provost.'

The woman stood frowning above them, so clearly mistress of the situation that the hearts of the two wanderers sank. The soul of Mr Stark, already raised high with vague belief in his comrade's dark and terrible designs, was genuinely alarmed by this shrewd reading of purpose. He looked to see Francis falter and stammer, and when he saw his face still calm and inscrutable, his voice yet unshaken, he bowed in spirit before a master.

As for Francis, he followed the broad path of denial.

'Hielandman or French,' he cried with a laugh. 'Is't like, think ye, when I haena a plack to spare I should take up my heid wi' beggars' politics? Na, na, a Whig am I and my faither afore me. I wadna stir my thoomb for a' the Charlies that ever whistled. Gin this were a change-house, mistress, and a bowl o' yill were on the board afore me, ye wad see me drink damnation to a' Pretenders, and health to King Geordie.'

His words were so violent and so honestly given that the woman looked momentarily satisfied. 'I've maybe mista'en ye,' she said; 'but at ony rate, whatever ye are, ye're shameless leears.'

'Maybe we are, gudewife,' said Francis, with ingratiating candour; 'but for us wandering men we never ken when we are wi' freends. The truth o' the maitter is that we cast oot wi' the captain, and have e'en ta'en the road to the west whaur we'll find another ship. Ye'll forgie us the lee, mistress?'

'Ye look like honest men,' said the woman, slowly and hesitatingly. 'You at ony rate,' and she turned to Francis. 'Ye've far ower long and sarious a face to be a blagyird.'

In the morning they were up betimes, and ready for the road. The shadow of Mr Berritch still hung over both, and a mist of suspicion was in the atmosphere of the dwelling. The final affront came at parting. Francis, with conscious honesty, offered payment for the night's lodging. The woman haggled and raised the price till she had all but angered him; then, with a hearty slap on the back, she bade him begone and live like an honest man. 'D'ye think,' said she, 'I wad tak payment frae twae forwandered callants? Gang your ways, man, and try gin ye can be as honest as ye're bonny.' And her laugh rang in his ears as he went down the street.

At first the glory of the morning set his spirits high. They were already on the western outskirts of the town, where the grey sea-beat tenements dwindle to outlying cottages which stare abruptly over meadowland and river. The September haze was rising in furling wisps before the wind, and the salt ocean air strove with the serener fragrance of shorn hayfields. There was something extraordinarily fresh and blithe in the wide landscape falling to the eye under the blue, and the bitter crispness of morn. Insensibly their limbs moved faster, they flung back their shoulders, and with open mouth and head erect drank in the life-giving air.

But as they plodded on, Francis soon fell into the clutches of memory, and his reflections pleased him little. The whole thought of the day before was full of irritation. On the threshold of high-handed adventure he had met with a closed door, and had been driven to a poverty-stricken compromise. Hitherto in dark moments of self-revelation he had buoyed himself with a flattering picture of a keen brain and a dauntless will. Now, both seemed to have failed grievously; he had been tricked and laughed at by a peddling sailor. Even the rhetorical parting did not comfort him.

Seen in the cold light of day it seemed crude and boyish. He could have torn his tongue out with rage when he thought on the grinning Mr Berritch and the gaping crew.

But more than this folly, he regretted his lapse from his first resolution. The fine renunciation of virtue which he had performed two nights before on the doorstep of his home was rapidly being made of no avail. He had been betrayed into compromise, into honesty. The words of the woman at Berwick still rang in his ears. She had clearly taken him for some truant apprentice, some temporary recreant from the respectable. The thought was gall and wormwood. He, the master, the scorner of the domestic, the Ulysses and Autolycus to be! And – alas for human consistency! – there was still another trouble of a vastly different kind. In one matter he was ashamed of deception. He had worn the badge of Whiggery in the eyes of Mr Stark, and though the need for the step had been apparent, he could not divest his mind of some faint scruples, the relics of an earlier ideal of gentility.

The result of such meditations was to drive the meditator into a bad temper, which he proceeded to vent on the ill-fated Starkie. This gentleman had spoken little, being filled with thoughts of his own. Somewhere in his curious nature was a strain of sentiment, which revelled in cheap emotions and the commonplaces of memory. The charms of Kate Mallison still held her fugitive lover, and as he travelled he lingered pleasantly over her face and figure, and formed his mouth to words of endearment. The virulence of his companion did not disturb him. For this he had made up his mind long ago. After all, if one seeks a great man as a friend, one must be prepared to bear with his humours. And when Francis, roused by memories of his fall into virtue, talked shrilly of desperate plans, Starkie inclined a deaf, yet willing ear, and went on with his fancies.

But by and by with the hours another feeling grew upon the elder's mind. The road ran among low birches with a sombre regiment of pines flanking it on the right. Through the spaces gleamed the sky, pale with the light haze of September, and on the left among reeds and willows twined and crooned the streams of Tweed. Francis was diverted against himself, and, ere ever he knew, the old glamour of the countryside had fallen upon him. He too, it was his proud reflection, was a son of this land, born of a family whose race was old as the hills and waters. The ancient nameless charm which slumbered with the green hillsides, flashed in the streams, and hung over the bare mosses, stole unbeknown into his soul, and the stout Francis was led captive by the poetry of the common world.

The mood lasted till near evening, when they slept at a little public somewhere by Leaderfoot. In the morn they were early awake, for those days of delay in their own land were irksome to both. Now they were in a stranger country, where hills came down to the water's edge, and the distance showed lines of blue mountain. The weather was still the placid and soothing warmth of a late summer, with roads running white and dry before them, and the quiet broken only by the sounds of leisured, rustic toil. For the nonce the bustling fervour died in Francis' breast, and he took his way through the gracious valley in a pleasant torpor of spirit.

But by midday, all this was driven to the winds by the conduct of Mr Stark. That gentleman, awakened from his sentiments of yesterday, fell to the purposeless chatter in which he specially excelled. Thence, finding his companion irresponsive, he glided naturally to the plotting of mischief. He had some desire to vindicate his name of adventurer in the eyes of his saturnine friend. So he cast about him for a fitting object.

Now ill luck sent him an opportunity at once too facile and too mean, for, when the pair stopped at a wayside cottage for water, he adroitly contrived to filch a cut of dried beef from the wooden dresser. In glee he showed it to Francis as they halted at midday a mile beyond. He expected approval, or at the least tolerance; but his reception sorely discomfited him, for to Francis the thing appeared so aimlessly childish, so petty, that his gorge rose at the sight. It was the act of a knavish boy, and the whole soul of this man of affairs was stirred to anger. If there was any flicker of honesty in the feeling it was sternly suppressed, but to the disgust he gave full rein.

'What for did ye do that?' he asked fiercely.

'Oh, juist to keep my hand in, belike,' said the Westlander.

'Ye damnable bairn,' cried Francis, 'd'ye call this a man's work, robbing auld wives of their meat, when ye have no need of it? I'll learn ye better. Come back with me, see, this minute, and if ye dinna pay her what she asks, you and me will quit company. D'ye think I will have ye running at my heels like a thieving collie?'

The elder man had too menacing a brow and angry tone for the feeble Mr Stark to resist. He followed him grumbling, and suffered himself to be led like a sheep within the cottage. The place was bare and poor; the woman, thin and white as a bone, and long fallen in the vale of years.

'My friend happened to lift something o' yours, mistress, and we e'en came to pay ye for it,' and Francis regarded the strange place with some pity.

'Were ye starvin', lads?' she asked in a piping voice, 'for if sae ye may keep the meat and welcome. But it would hae been mair faisable to speir.'

But, try they their best, she would take no payment, and they had to leave in despair. The thing put both into an ill humour. Starkie nursed a grievance, and Francis had much the same temper as the Christian who laments the failure of judgment upon the wicked. They spoke no words, but stalked silently on different sides of the road, with averted eyes and tragic bearing.

But continued surliness was little in Starkie's way. At the end of half an hour he was jocose and making farcical overtures to friendship. When he found his efforts repulsed, he comforted himself with a song, and when in a little they came to a village and a public, turned gladly to the relief of drink. Now, whether it was that the landlord's ale had extraordinary qualities or that Starkie drank a wondrous amount, it is certain that ere he had gone far it became clear that he was grossly drunk.

Thence the course of the two became troubled and uncertain. Starkie drew up to the other in maudlin amity. Francis had drunk little and his gloomy temper still held. He had never loved drunkenness, and at the moment his thoughts dwelt on the failure of his plans. So he sent Mr Stark to the devil with no mincing words. With drunken gravity Starkie retorted, and then with more drunken heroism squared himself to fight. The patience of Francis fairly gave way. Gripping his assailant by the collar and breeches he tossed him easily to the roadside.

'Lie there, ye drunken swine,' he cried, 'and I'm glad I'm quit o' ye.'

So, pursued by thickly uttered reproaches, he hastened forward alone.

With the next dawn Francis found himself on the confines of great hills, where the river, now shrunk to a stream, foamed in a narrow vale. The weather had changed with the night to cloud and cold, and the even drizzle of a Scots mist obscured the sun. The slopes gloomed black and wet, every burn was red with flood, and the sparse trees dripped in dreary silence. The place was singularly dispiriting, for naught met the eye but the mire underfoot and the murky folds of mist.

Early in the day he stopped a passing shepherd and asked him his whereabouts. He was told with great wealth of detail which further befogged his mind. Then on a sudden impulse he asked where lay Yarrow and the Birkenshaw Tower. 'D'ye see that hill ower the water?' was the answer. 'That's the Grey Drannock, and the far side o't looks straucht doun on the Yarrow water.' This then was the confines of his own land, these were haply his forefathers' hills; a sudden pride went through his heart, but the next moment he was looking drearily on his lamentable fortunes.

He was sick of himself, disgusted with his ill-success, and half inclined to rue his parting with Mr Stark. Where were his fine resolutions? All vanishing into air under the blast of his spasmodic virtues. As he looked back on the events of the past days he was driven by his present sourness especially to loathe his flashes of decency. The dismal weather helped to harden him. After all, he reflected, the world is a battleground, where he wins who is least saddled with the baggage of virtue. Man preys upon man; I may expect no mercy from others; and none shall others get from me. So it was with fierce purpose and acrid temper that Francis travelled through the clammy weather. It had been Starkie, he thought with irritation, and not himself that had the true spirit; and he cursed the hour when he had left the little Westlander in the ditch.

By the evening it cleared and the sun set stormily over monstrous blue hills. He had passed through the town of Peebles in the early afternoon, and now followed the western road up the green pastoral dale of the upper Tweed. The dusk was drawing in as he left the river and took the path which ran to Ayr by Lanark and Clyde. Just at the darkening the lights of a little village beckoned him – a line of white houses and a cluster of rowans by a burnside. His legs were growing weary, and he had not yet supped; so he turned to the inn to bide the night.

FIVE

The Portrait of a Lady

In such rough and casual fashion Francis came to his Destiny. But to him there was little sign of aught momentous. The inn kitchen was half-filled with men talking, while the landlord's deep tones gave directions to the serving-girl. The noise of soft South-country talk came pleasantly on his ears after the clip-clap of the Fife, and a wholesome smell of food and drink comforted his senses.

He sat by himself in a corner, for he was in the mood to shun publicity. Supper was brought him, and then he stretched his legs to the fire, since already the evenings grew chilly. In this lethargic comfort his follies ceased to trouble him, and he tasted the delights of wearied ease.

But as the hour grew late the room cleared, and Francis awoke to interest in his surroundings. He asked the landlord what the place might be.

He was told, 'Brochtoun.'

The name stuck in his memory. Broughton – he had heard it somewhere, linked with some name which had slipped his recollection. He asked who owned the land.

'Murray,' was the answer, 'Murray o' Brochtoun, kin to them o' Stanhope. A graceless lot, aye plottin' and conspirin' wi' them that's better no named. Even now him and his leddy wife are awa to the North, trokin' wi' the wild Jaicobites and French.' The landlord's politics were clear and vehement.

At the word Francis sat up in earnest. Murray of Broughton was already a noted name in the land, the catchword of the whole tribe of needy loyalists, the confidant and companion of the Prince himself and in every Edinburgh tavern he had heard the toast of the beautiful Mrs Murray given with drunken leers and unedifying tales. If all stories were true, she was a lady of uncommon parts and spirit and not too nice a conscience. This, then, was the home of the Murrays on which he, the out-at-elbows adventurer, had stumbled. As he thought of himself he felt a singular antipathy to this tribe of aristocrats – doubtless filled with pride of race and the fantastic notions of honour from which he had parted forever.

The thought had scarce left him when a man who had been sitting at the door came up and touched his sleeve from behind. He turned to find a face familiar to him – a little man with ferret eyes and bushy eyebrows, poverty staring from the rents in his coat. He knew him for a chance acquaintance in that lowest deep of city life to which he had made some few excursions.

'D'ye no mind me?' said the man eagerly.

'I've seen ye before,' said Francis ungraciously.

'Dod Craik,' said the man, 'I'm Dod Craik. Ye mind Dod Craik. I've seen ye at the Pirliewow and M'Gowks and the Three Herrins, and, d'ye no mind, ye aince betted me twa crouns I couldna find my way across the street ae nicht when I was blind-fou. Ay, and I stottit the hale length o' that lang vennel and fell under a bailie's coach and was ta'en aff to jail.' And the wretched creature laughed with the humour of it.

'Well, supposing I mind you, Mr Craik,' said the unbending Francis, 'I'll trouble ye to tell me what ye want. If it's siller, ye'll get none from me, for I'm as toom as a kirk plate.'

'It's no siller,' cried the man. 'Na, na, from a' I hear ye're just a venturer like mysel'. But it's a thing wi' siller in't, and I thocht ye micht like to hae a finger in the job.'

The notion pleased, and Francis held out a relenting hand to the little man. 'If that's your talk, Mr Craik, then I am with you.'

'Then maybe ye could step ootside wi' me for the maitter o' a few meenutes,' said the other, and the two went forth into the street.

The man led Francis out of the light of the houses into the gloom of the birk-lined road. 'I kenned aye ye were a man o' speerit and withoot prejudices, Mr Birkenshaw,' he began.

'Let my spirit and prejudices alone,' said Francis shortly.

'And wi' nae scruples how ye cam by money if aince ye but had it.'

'Man, will ye come to the point?' said Francis, who was in doubt whether to be pleased or angry at this narration of attributes.

'Weel, it's this. The hoose o' Brochtoun is standin' toom or as guid as toom, save for a servant or twae. It's kenned that Murray is in league wi' rebels and has the keepin' o' their gold. It's beyond credibeelity that he can hae ta'en it to the North wi' him, so it maun be left here. Now I propose that you and me as guid subjects o' the King find a road intil the hoose and lay our hands on thae ill-gotten gains. I've lang had this ploy in my heid, and I had trysted wi' anither man for the nicht, but he's failed me. The short and lang o' the maitter is that the job's ower big for ae man, so when I got a glisk o' ye, I made up my mind to gie ye the chance.' He waited nervously for the answer.

Francis flushed for the moment. 'D'ye ken what ye ask me to do, Mr Craik?' said he. 'It's a job that some folk would call house-breaking and stouthrief.'

'Na,' said the other, 'it's no that. It's the lawfu' consequence o' poeetical principles. Think ye, if the sodgers in Embro had word o' siccan a thing they wadna be the first to tak it? If ye believe me, Mr Birkenshaw, it's a naational necessity.'

'But what do ye ken of my principles?' asked Francis. 'Who telled ye I wasna as hot a Jacobite as Murray himself?'

The man looked shrewdly at his neighbour to detect his purpose. Then he laughed incredulously. 'Gae awa wi' ye and your havers. Ye were aye ower fond o' a saft seat and a bieldy corner.'

For a little Francis hesitated, in two minds whether to join forces with this house-breaker or there and then to give him the soundest of thrashings. His parting with Starkie still rankled in his mind. He called up the designs which he had formed for himself, his abhorrence of trivial virtue, his deification of the unscrupulous. This was a chance both to better his means and restore his confidence. This would be the rubicon over which there was no returning to the dreary paths of the respectable. His course was clear, and yet with a vanishing pride he could have beaten this little city blackguard who called him companion.

So he told Mr Craik of his compliance, and was rewarded with a sigh of relief. 'Man, I kenned ye wad dae't, and noo we're shure o' success. Come down the road till I tell ye the ways o't. I've been hereabouts for days till I ken ilka turn o' the place. The hoose looks north ower a dean o' trees and a' to the south is the whinny back o' a hill. There's naether windy nor door kept lockit the noo on that gairden side, for at a' hoors there's a steer o' men comin' and leavin'.' And with a crowd of such directions he led him into the shade.

It was clear that Murray's folk had small liking for their laird. There in the inn sat Whiggery triumphant, smiled upon by a Calvinist landlord and a score of staunch Presbyterian followers. Farther down the water the Cause found many adherents, but there, on the very confines of the West, there was something dour and covenanting in the air, and the fervours of the master and his lady awoke no answer among the men of Broughton. Had two such characters as Mr Craik and Francis been seen in an Atholl or Badenoch inn they would have been jealously spied upon; but there they were suffered to go their ways, and in a corner of the kitchen over their glasses they brought the project to completion.

An hour later the two men were climbing the brae which rose from the green haughs of the burn to the upland valley where stood the house. Francis had the same free stride as ever, but Mr Craik hastened over the brighter patches of moonlight and stole gladly to the shadows. To himself Francis seemed something less worthy than before. The mist of daring and escapade, with which he fancied his course to be shrouded, had begun to disappear under the cold north wind of Mr Craik's company. He had set out on the ploy for money and self-satisfaction; but soon he wished that he had come alone, for his disgust rose at the sight of the ferret-faced thing which led him.

Soon they were on the bare hill-face and looking down upon

the back windows of the dwelling. To the left there was light in the lower windows, where probably dwelt the few domestics, but otherwise the whole of the great wall was black with darkness. Mr Craik chuckled joyfully and led the way across the garden fence and down an alley of flowers. At the edge of the lawn he stopped and held a whispered consultation.

'That windy forenent us is never barred; the lock's broke, for I was up last nicht to find oot. Now if ye gang in there ye come to a passage which takes ye to the maister's ain room. It's no the first door but the second on the left-hand side, and there he keeps his siller and valuables. It's aye lockit, but I've trystit wi' a servant lass to leave the key in the door. Aince ye won there, ye wad lock the thing on the inside and search the place at your leesure. Syne ye wad come back to me and I wad help ye oot. The reason why twae men's needit is that the windy canna open frae within, and if there werna ane oot bye to lift it, there wad be nae mainner o' escape. Now, whilk is to gang and whilk is to bide?' and he took a coin from his pocket to toss.

'Ye'd better let me try it,' said Francis. 'I'm bigger and stronger, and maybe I've a better eye for a hidy-hole.' Already he was beginning to loathe the business, and chose this part of it as the less discreditable. It was better to have his hand at the work than to wait outside like a child.

'Man, ye've speerit,' said the other admiringly and not without gratitude. Fear had already begun to wrestle with his avarice.

So Francis raised the window, which fitted like a portcullis into a socket above. His companion held it open till his long legs had struggled through. He found himself in a narrow corridor, pitchy dark, save for the glimmer from the window. A musty smell, as of an old and little-used house, hung all about it, and his groping feet detected an uneven floor. An utter silence prevailed, in which as from a great distance he heard the click of the shut window.

He felt with his hand along the left wall. One door he passed, of stout ribbed oak securely fastened. Then the place widened, and he seemed to be in a hall with some kind of matting upon the floor. Here his feet went noiselessly, and a faint degree of light obtained from a window far in front. Then his hand came on the space of a second door, and he stopped to test it. This was clearly the place where the key was to be found, as Mr Craik had directed.

But it was no less closely bolted than the last, and the keyhole was empty. He put his shoulders to the panel and shook it. He heard only the rasp of a great lock in its place, but the door did not give an inch. Again he tried, and this time the woodwork cracked. But the noise warned him, echoing in that still place with double power, and he desisted.

Nothing remained but to try elsewhere, so he groped farther down the hall. Again he touched a handle, and this time with better success; for to his amazement he found the door ajar, and pushing it open entered a wide room. He turned to look for a key, but found none; this, too, was not the place appointed; but since he had found an entrance he resolved to go farther. The place was black with night. A dim haze of light seemed to hang at the end, which doubtless came from a shuttered window. As he groped his way he stumbled on furniture which felt rich and softly draped to the touch. A faint odour of food, too, lurked in the air, as if the room had been used for dining.

This was not the goal which he had sought, but even here something might be found. So Francis was in the act of beginning a hasty scrutiny when a sound brought him to a stop. A footstep was crossing the hall and making for the room. A pioneer ray of light gleamed below the door. He was in a quandary, uncertain whither to turn; he could not flee by the door, and no other way was apparent. To hide behind some curtain or cabinet was possible, and he was about to creep hastily to the back when a hand was laid on the latch. Some instinct prompted him to sink quietly into a chair and wait the issue.

The light of a lamp flooded the room, showing its noble size and costly furnishing. Francis sat silent in his chair, curious of the result, and busily searching his brains for some plausible tale. The light-bearer saw at the table-end a long man, his face dark with the sun, dressed decently yet with marks of travel, and bearing somewhere in his dress and demeanour the stamp of a townsman, who sat waiting on the newcomer's question with eyes half apologetic and half bold.

As for Francis himself, he saw a vision which left him dumb. He had expected the sight of a servant or at most some gentleman of the Cause using the house as a lodging. But to his wonder, in the doorway stood a woman holding a lamp above her and looking full from its canopy of light into the half-darkness. In the dimness she seemed tall and full of grace, standing alert and stately with a great air of queenship. Her gown was of soft white satin, falling in shining folds to her feet, and showing the tender curves of arm and bosom. Above, at the throat and wrists, her skin was white as milk, and the hair rose in dark masses on her head, framing her wonderful face – pale with the delicate paleness so far above roses. Something in her eye, in the haughty carriage of the little head, in the life and grace which lay in every curve and motion, took suddenly from Francis the power of thought. He looked in silent amazement at this goddess from the void.

He had waited for surprise, anger, even fear; but to his wonder he found only recognition. She looked on him as if she had come there for no other purpose than to seek him. A kindly condescension, the large condescension of one born to rule and be obeyed, was in her demeanour.

'Ah, you are here,' she said. 'I thought you had not come. You are my Lord Manorwater's servant?'

For an instant Francis' wits wandered at the suddenness of the question. Then his readiness returned, and he grasped the state of matters. He rose hurriedly to his feet and bowed. 'I have that honour, my lady,' said he; and he reflected that his sober dress would suit the character.

As he stood a tumult of thoughts rushed through his brain. This was the famous lady whom he had so often heard of, she who was the Cause, the Prince, and the King to so many loyal gentlemen. His eyes gloried in her beauty, for somewhere in his hard nature there was an ecstatic joy in mere loveliness. But the bodily perfection was but a drop in the cup of his astonishment. She had clearly been receiving guests in this old house, and guests of quality, for the rich white gown was like a state dress, and jewels flashed at her neck and fingers. A swift and violent longing seized him to be one of her company, to see her before him, to be called her friend. In her delicate grace she seemed the type of all he had renounced forever – nay, not renounced, for in his turbid boyhood he had had no glimpse of it. To this wandering and lawless man for one second the elegancies of life were filled with charm, and he sighed after the unattainable. Then his mood changed to one of fierce revulsion. This was a lady of rank and wealth, doubtless with a crazy pride of place and honour, condescending gravely to him as to one far beneath; and he, he was the careless, the indomitable, who would yet laugh in the face of the whole orderly world.

But such sentimental reflections were soon succeeded by thoughts more practical. He had run his head into a difficult place, and might yet escape by this lucky chance which called him a servant of Lord Manorwater's. But there was little time to lose, lest the real lackey should come to confront him. His ready brain was already busy with plans when the lady spoke again.

'Your master will have told you your errand. This is the letter which I desire you to carry and put into the hands of Mr Murray of Broughton at his lodging in the Northgate of Edinburgh. Your master told me you have travelled the same road before to the same place.'

Francis said 'Ay.'

'Then I have but one word for you. Take the hills from here and keep off the highroad, above all near the inn of Leidburn. For I have heard tonight that a body of rebel soldiers is lying there. When you come to my husband, he will give you his directions, whether to go with him and the royal army or to return here. But in any case I can trust the diligence and loyalty of one of my Lord Manorwater's men.' And she smiled on him graciously.

'And they brought you in here and left you in darkness,' she said, as if in self-reproach. 'It is a hard thing to live in such troubled times. And perhaps you have not supped?'

Francis protested that he had already had food, in mortal fear lest she should delay him with refreshment.

'I will let you out myself,' she said, and lifting the lamp she led the way from the room, her soft skirts trailing and the light flickering on her dusky hair. Francis followed in a fervour of delight. The sudden vista of a great plan had driven all sentiment from his mind. Now at last he might get free of petty ill-doing, and exercise his wits on matters of greater import. He carried a letter which meant money from any officer of Government; he scented plot and intrigue all richly flavoured with peril. He felt himself no more the casual amateur, but the established schemer, meddling with the affairs of nations. The thought restored him to his perverted self-respect.

She opened the hall door and let him pass into the park with a word of good-speed. As he departed he turned for a moment, and his sentiment flickered to life, for as she stood, a radiant figure of light in the arch of the door, his mind reverted to this great loveliness.

But a second later such thoughts had fled, and with no care for the patient Mr Craik waiting silently by the back window, Francis took his path for the highway and the Leidburn inn.

SIX

On the Edinburgh Highway

The moon was up, whitening the long highway to the north, as Francis sped gaily on. It was still early night; lengthy hours were to come before the dawn; and Leidburn inn was no more than a dozen miles. But the exhilaration of escape, of new hope, drove him with eager legs, and he watched the trees fall away and the barer hills draw together with pride in his fleet strength.

At the watershed the moors stretched dim and yellow on either hand in a melancholy desolation. A curlew piped on the bent, and then all was still as the grave but for the clack of his shoes on the hill gravel. He fell out of his run and took to the stride with which he had been wont to stalk through the back vennels of the city. The soft odours of moorland weather hung about the place as over a shrine. The luminous sky above had scarcely a hint of dark, but shone like an ocean starred with windy isles in some twilight of the gods.

His first resolution had grown and made itself clear in every part. He pictured gleefully the incidents of his course. The soldiers found, he called for their Captain and delivered his letter. The tide of war was turned, he was honoured with reward, and a life of bold intrigue awaited him. Exultantly he pictured his fate – how the world would some day talk of him with fear, how his name would be on all men's lips and his terror in every heart. Then haply Mr Francis Birkenshaw would set his heel on the neck of his oppressors.

But his importunate commonsense drew him sharply back from his flights. It meant but a guinea for his pocket and a glass of wine for his thirst, for he could only pose as a lackey if he wished for credence. Yet even in this there was promise. It needed but his wits and his habitual bold presence to push his fortune far. Here, in his own land, lay his field. Far better to seize a spoke of Fate's wheel as she twirled it here than hunt the jade in lands oversea.

The way led him through a bogland meadow and up again to the skirts of a hill. In a little he was among trees, whence came the chilly echo of running water and a gleam of light from some sequestered dwelling. Already a wider vale seemed to open and high, dark hill-shapes rose on the left. The road was wide and even, for by it men chiefly travelled to Carlisle and the South. Even as he sped a rumble of wheels came to his ear, and he was in the roadside heather watching a four-horse carriage go by. The horses seemed weary with forcing, and within the coach by the moonlight he had a glimpse of anxious faces. Lord Smitwood, or the great Lady Blaecastle, or the famous Mrs Maxwell, he thought, on their way to put their sundry houses in order against an evil day. Clearly wars and rumours of war were thickening in the North, and he was soon to have a hand in the game.

And with this he fell back on thoughts of Broughton and the lady of the Jacotot lace and dusky hair. Something in her image as it flashed on his memory roused keen exaltation. He would trick this proud woman and all her kind, crush them, use them for his purpose. Each feature, as he reflected on it, roused his hatred. She was fair; well, beauty for the joy of the strong. Men said she was clever; well, he would match her with counter-wits and gain the victory. Three hours before, and he had never seen her; now she filled his whole fancy with her hateful beauty. He thought of her freely, grossly, as he had trained himself to think of women. But somewhere in the man there was a string of fine sentiment which jarred at the incongruous. The exquisite freshness of her beauty forbade her a place in a gallery of harlots, and to his disgust he found himself forced to regard her with decency.

The thing stuck in his memory and began to vex him. Vigorously he questioned himself if he were not falling back to boyish virtue. Reassured by the hot and lustful spirit within him, he searched for some catchword or badge of his resolve.

So all the latter part of the way he hummed rags of ill-reputed ditties, and now and then in the near neighbourhood of a cottage made the night hideous with a tune. For he was now at the verge of settled country, where King George held a tight rein, and no loyalist gentry would be at hand with a bullet from the wayside. So leisurely had been his course that the autumn dawn was already breaking ere he rounded the hill and came out on the level Leidburn moss. The place was desert – acres of peat with the film of morn still raw on the heather, and the black reaches of a lazy stream. But through the midst ran the fresh-coloured highway, and there, half a mile distant, rose the white walls of the inn. Even as he walked the thin air of dawn brought him the noise of hens' cackling and the first stir of life. Beyond all there stretched a great wide country of meadow and woodland to the horizon of the morning, the smoke of a city and the broad curve of the sea.

The scene was so airy and clear that Francis fell into good humour with himself, and drew near to the inn with pleasant confidence. He had expected to find some traces of the military, some neighing from the stable or bustle of servants, but to his wonder the house was silent. The kitchen door stood open, and through it he passed with the appearance of a lackey's haste.

'Landlord,' he cried, in a voice of importance, and a heavy man came down a trap-stair from a garret. Francis' manner assumed the ease of politeness and good-fellowship mingled. 'I have word for the Captain,' he said, 'and I maun see him before I hae my breakfast. But quick, man, get something ready for me.'

'The Captain!' the landlord cried with disgust, 'and whatna Captain, my lad? I've had eneuch o' captains in thae fower walls this last week to mak hell ower thrang for the deil himsel'. But they're a' cleared noo, gone yestreen the last o' them to fecht the Hielandmen. God, I wish them luck. They'll find a Hieland cateran's dirkie a wee bit less pleasin' in their wames than my guid bannocks.'

Here was news of vexation. 'But where have they gone, and can I no meet up wi' them?' he asked.

'It's easy to tell that,' said the sarcastic host. 'They're just in Embro and nae farther. Cope has landed some way doun the Firth, and a' King George's lads are drawing to that airt. They say the Chevalier and his Hielanders gang oot the day to meet them. Weary fa' them for spoilin' an honest man's trade! Fechtin' tae wi'oot breeks and wi' nae skeel in pouther and leid! God!' And the man laughed deep and silent.

'The Chevalier?' Francis stammered.

'Ay, the Chevalier,' said the man. 'Whaur hae ye been wanderin' a' thae days that ye havena heard o' him? Chairlie's king o' the castle the day, though he may be doun wi' a broken croun the morn.'

'I have been long in the South,' said Francis hastily, 'and forbye, I am given to doing my ain business and no heeding the clash of the country.'

'Weel, weel, maybe sae. But if I were your maister, my lad, I wad pick ane mair gleg at the uptak than yoursel'.' And the landlord went off, rolling with his heavy gait, to fetch the stranger breakfast.

Francis sat down to reflect on this state of matters with some philosophy. It meant a longer journey for himself ere he disposed of his business, and a greater risk of frustration. He thought for a moment of playing the faithful messenger after all, and casting his services at the Secretary's feet. But the thought was scarce serious, for with it came the unpleasant consideration that his position would still be a lackey's, and that he would be likely to have difficulties if he ever came within range of Lord Manorwater or the Secretary's wife. Soon he was reconciled even to the twenty-odd miles which still awaited him, for the holding of Edinburgh and the coming of the English general meant a crisis of war, when news would be bought and sold at a higher price. But he must be wary and quick, or any wandering loyalist might trick him. So he cried to the landlord to hurry the meal, and stretched his already wearied legs in a chair.

'Are ye for Embro?' asked the landlord.

'Even so,' said Francis guilelessly, 'since ye say the Captain is there.'

'Ye'll hae a gey wark finding him, my lad,' said the other. 'Captains will be as thick as fleas in Embro the noo, and the maist o' them withoot the breeks. If ye're wise ye'll look for the man ye're seekin' mair east the country on the road to join the ithers. What did ye say was his name?'

'I wasna told any name,' said Francis, feeling himself on the edge of a hazard. 'A' I got was "The Captain at Leidburn inn".'

The landlord laughed. 'They keep ye muckle in the dark on your side tae. I had thocht that that wark was left for the Hielandmen.'

'What side do ye incline to yoursel'?' asked Francis.

'Nae side,' said the man shortly. 'I treat a' the warld as my customers, whether they wear the breeks or no. But my faither was ane o' the Cameronian kind, and I'm half persuaded that way mysel'.'

But at this moment a rattle at the door proclaimed another visitor. Francis turned anxious eyes, for might not this be some servant of the Murrays or Manorwaters? But the sight of the newcomer reassured him, for there in all the dust of travel and abandon of weariness stood the deserted Starkie.

He had not prospered in these last days, for his clothing was much soiled and his face was lean with exertion. He fell back at the sight of his aforetime comrade, as if doubtful of his reception. But Francis was in the humour in which to hail his arrival with delight. Yesterday he had repented his loss, and now he was in a mood to atone for it. He greeted him with a cry of pleasure, and drew the hesitating Westlander to the fire.

'We've foregathered again,' said he, 'and now we'll be the better friends. In these stirring times, Mr Stark, there's no room for ill nature.'

'And I'm glad to see ye, Mr Birkenshaw, for I have missed ye sair. God, I'll ne'er forget that weary wander ower the Tweed hills. I've been a' airts but the right yin since I saw ye.'

Both ate their breakfast ravenously, while mutual questioning filled the pauses. As they talked, the anomaly of their course came forcibly before each mind, and each asked the reason of this unexpected meeting-place.

'What brought ye to these parts, Starkie? This is no road to Clyde and the West.'

'Oh, I've nae doubt it was the same reason as yoursel'. When I came bye the top o' Tweed the hale land was turned upside doun wi' rumours o' war, and ilka plooman gettin' his musket. They telled me Embro was gotten by the Prince, and that a' the brave lads were rinnin' to his flag. So, thinks I, I may as weel try my luck in my ain land as in the abroad. Forbye, I'll pay out my faither, for gin he heard o' siccan daein's he wad gang out o' his mind. He bides ower near the Hieland Line to love the Hielandmen. But if ye've nae objections, I wad like to hear what brocht you yersel' this gate.'

'Wheesht, Starkie,' said Francis, looking darkly at the land-lord, 'I've a ploy on hand to make both our fortunes.' And he watched the host till he had betaken himself to the far back of the kitchen. Then he leaned forward and tapped his companion on the arm. 'Starkie, man, I have a letter.'

The Westlander's eyes brightened. 'That's guid, and whae is it frae?'

'From the Secretary's wife to the Secretary's self.'

The announcement was made in stage tones and received with proper awe. 'Mr Birkenshaw, ye're great,' said Starkie, and Francis' vanity was appeased. It had been somewhat wounded by the independent tone which his companion had seen fit to assume since their severance.

Then in brief words he proceeded to unfold his plans. He would make straight for the east end of the Firth, and meet the Government leaders. The near crisis of the war would heighten his value and gain him favour. He had heard enough of the Prince's men to have little faith in them; time would soon work their ruin; and then would come reward for the loyal adherent. Starkie listened and approved, so both in their ignorance saw a roseate horizon to their policy.

But the businesslike Westland mind had one addendum. The letter might be of the highest consequence; again it might be a trifle, which would merely expose the bearer to contempt. It would be well to inquire into its contents.

Francis pondered, hesitated, and then blankly refused. Something, he knew not what, held him from opening it. He scouted the idea of honour – that was flung far behind – but a sense of fitness even in the details of roguery was strong upon him. He had still some memory of the hands from which he had got the letter, and his sentiment had not utterly flown. The feeling might permit high, audacious treachery, but not so small a piece of bad faith. He was on the verge of the humour in which two days before he had flung his companion into the ditch.

In his luckless way Starkie ministered to the growing repulsion. The thought of the future delighted him, and he hastened to sketch its details. Alike in his childishness and his flashes of shrewdness he was repugnant to the maturer Francis. His view of the conduct of affairs was so plainly ingenuous that it filled the other with despair, and his idea of happiness was the craziest mixture of the respectable and sillily wicked. Francis, still in the heat of a great plan, with his brain yet fired from the deeds of the night before, had no tolerance for such a huckstering paradise.

From ill temper the two were rapidly drifting to a quarrel. These last days had found Starkie some independence, and he was scarcely disposed to bear with his comrade's megrims. He assumed a tone of consequence, and replied to Francis' gibes with flat rustic retorts. The landlord came up betimes and tried in vain to mediate. Francis had the grace to hold his peace, but not so the other. He sank from vituperation to complaint, and was on the verge of confiding all grievances to the open ears of the host.

Meanwhile the hours were passing, and a hot blaze of sun in the windows warned Francis that he must soon be stirring. For a second he was tempted to leave his companion then and there, but he curbed his irritation with the bridle of policy and reflected on his probable usefulness. He was in the act of conciliating him by timely concession – by falling in with the tune of his hopes and throwing him crumbs of flattery – when a noise of hooves and wheels sounded without on the road and then stopped short at the inn door.

Both men sprang to their feet, while the landlord hurried to clear the table. A woman's voice was heard as if giving orders, and then a step on the threshold, and the door was opened. The blinking eyes of Mr Stark saw a lady, tall and fair, in a travelling cloak of dark velvet, with a postilion at her back. But Francis' breath stopped in his throat, for he knew the face of the woman he was playing false to.

'Landlord,' she cried in her clear high voice, 'the off wheeler has gone lame, and I must be in Edinburgh in an hour. Quick, get me a fresh beast, and have the other looked to.' Then, as she haughtily cast her eyes around the place, she caught sight of the gaping Starkie and Lord Manorwater's trusted servant. For a second her face looked bewilderment; then a quick gleam of comprehension entered, and her cheeks grew hot with anger.

'So,' said she, 'I have found you out, you cur. You thought to trick me with your tales and professions. Doubtless you are now on your way to your own master with your news. Perhaps it will please you to know that it is valueless, since the Prince's army has taken the field. It was well that I warned you against this place, else I might have missed this proof of your fidelity. Truly my Lord Manorwater is happy in his servants.'

Plainly she still took him for a lackey, and the thought added gall to his discomfiture. To be defeated in bold treachery was bad, but to stand condemned as a lying menial was bitter to a man's pride. For a second he tried to brazen it, but his overpowering vexation made him quail before her eyes.

But now the landlord spoke out in his harsh voice—

'You will get nae horse frae my stable, my leddy. I am a King's man, and will see you and your Prince in hell ere I stir a fit to help. Ye maun e'en gang farther and try your luck, mistress.'

'Do you refuse?' she cried. 'Then by Heaven, I will take it

myself, and lash you round your own yard. I will burn the place over your head ere the week is out, and then you may have leisure to repent your incivility.'

The fierce rhetoric of her tone cowed the recalcitrant host, but he had no time for a second thought. 'Robin,' she turned to her man, 'you will get the horse while I wait here and talk to these gentlemen. But, see, give me your whip. I shall have need of it.'

The fellow went, and she turned again to the three astounded spectators.

'Stop! What the –' cried the landlord, but she checked him with uplifted arm. 'I have no ill-will to you,' she said, 'and would prevent you from doing yourself a hurt. I am the wife of the Secretary Murray, and you will find me hard to gainsay. So I beg you to keep out of my quarrel.'

Then she turned once more to the pair with her intolerable scorn.

'And you are men,' she cried, 'made in the likeness of those who are fighting at this hour for their honour and King, while you cower in an alehouse and lay plots for women. But, bah! I waste words on you. Angry words are for men, but a whip for servants. You pair of dumb dogs, you will get a dog's punishment.' And she struck Francis full in the face with her lash.

At the first crack of the whip, Starkie with the instinct of his kind made for the door, and had the fortune to escape. He had no stomach to encounter this avenging Amazon with her terrible words and more terrible beauty. But Francis stood immovable, his mind crushed and writhing, his cheeks flaming with disgrace. This bright creature before him had tumbled his palace of cards about his ears. He felt with acid bitterness the full ignominy, the childish, servile shame of his position. The charm of her young beauty drove him frantic; her whole mien, as of a world unknown to him and eternally beyond his reach, mocked him to despair. For a moment he was the blacksmith's grandson, with the thought to rush forward, wrest the whip from her hands, and discomfit this proud woman with his superior strength. But some tincture of the Birkenshaw blood held him back. In that instant he knew the feebleness of his renunciation of virtue. Some power not himself forbade the extremes of disgrace – some bequest from more gallant fore-bears, some lingering wisp of honour. He stood with bowed head, not daring to meet her arrogant eyes, careless of the lash which curled round his cheek and scarred his brow. Marvellous the power of that slender arm! He felt the blood trickle over his eyes and half blind him, but he scarce had a thought of pain.

Then she flung down the whip on the floor.

'Go,' she cried, 'I am done with you. You may think twice before you try the like again.'

He moved dumbly to the door, and as he passed lifted his eyes suddenly to her face. Dimly he saw that her gaze was fixed on his bleeding forehead, and in her look he seemed to see a gleam of pity and at her mouth a quiver of regret. Then with crazy speed he ran blindly to the open moor.

SEVEN

Of a Lady on a Grey Horse

The sun was far up in the sky and the world lay bathed in the clear light of noon. The long rough expanse of bog lay flat before him with its links of moss-pools and great hags of peat. But he ran as on open ground, leaping the water, springing from tussock to tussock of heather, with his cheeks aflame and his teeth set in his lips. He drove all thoughts from his mind; the bitterness of shame weighed upon him like a mount of lead; when he looked back at times and saw the inn still in view, the sight maddened him to greater speed. So keen was his discomfiture that he scarcely felt weariness, though he had been travelling for a day and a night, with no sleep. When at last he came to the limit of the desert and emerged on fields of turf he ran the faster, till a ridge of hill hid the hateful place from his sight, and he sank on the ground.

In a little he sat up, for though utterly tired his whirling brain did not suffer him to rest. Now, when the scene of his disgrace was no more before his eyes, he strove to take the edge from his mental discomfort. Drearily he conjured back every detail, and for a little it seemed as if his shame would be driven out by the more bearable passion of anger. But the attempt failed lamentably. He had wholly lost his old sentiment of bravado; he saw his flimsy schemes wither before the bright avenging presence and himself a mere knavish servant in her eyes. In his misery the sight of her obstructed all his vision. At one moment he hated her with deadly vehemence; at the next he would have undergone all humiliation for a sight of her face. The inflated romance which had first driven him out on his travels was centred for the time on this one woman, and with it there followed the bitterness of despair.

Then he feebly clutched at his wits and set himself to review his position. It was black, black, without a tincture of hope. He had failed in his treachery, and something within him made him dimly conscious that this form of roguery was somehow or other shut to him henceforth. The role of the high-handed adventurer could not be his; even in a simple matter how dismally he had failed. And yet he could scarcely regret it, for at the moment the part had lost its charm. He must follow his first intentions and sail abroad, but with what altered hopes and spirit! For at that hour Mr Francis Birkenshaw in his youth and strength felt that already he was verging on the dull confines of age. But with it all the thought of that foreign journey was unpleasing. He had ruined his life in his own land, but yet he was loth to leave it, for the vague sentiment which was working in his heart was all associated with this barren country and the impending wars. He had the sudden thought that his services might still be worth their price in either army, but, again, he found no comfort. King George's forces, alien in race and unglorified by any fantastic purpose, did not attract him; the other side was a dream, a chimera, and moreover his breach of faith had cut him off from it forever. An acceptable recruit he would appear, when Murray of Broughton was leader!

So with hopeless purpose he set out over the well-tilled country for the shores of the Firth. This new ferment would make Edinburgh as safe for him as a foreign city, and it was an easier task to sail from the Firth than from a western port. He tried hard to recover his attitude of scorn for fate and firm self-confidence. But it was little use. No casuistry could persuade him to see his folly in a brighter light; he had lost his grip on the world, and now was driven about like a leaf where aforetime he had purposed to hew a path.

It was well on in the afternoon ere he struck a track, for he had taken his course at right angles to the main highway and found himself mazed in a country of sheepwalks. Thence the road ran down into a broad lowland vale, set with clumps of wood and smoking houses, with a gleam of water afar among low meadows. Autumn was tingeing leaf and stalk, and her blue haze rimmed the farthest trees and the line of abrupt hills. But the golden afternoon had no soothing effect upon him; he saw all things in the light of his own grey future, and plodded on with bent head and weary footstep. The effects of his toil, too, were beginning to come over him, and he found himself at times dizzy and all but fainting. The few people he met – farmers with carts, packmen, and a half-dozen country lasses – looked curiously at the tall dishevelled man with his weather-stained clothing. He stopped no one to ask the way, for the road ran clear to the city, and at its high places gave a prospect of roofs and steeples against the silver of the Firth. But sleep overcame him before nightfall, and he had to content himself with a lodging in the nearest village.

This he found to be a straggling place with one great inn in the middle, and a little church in a wood of birches at the end. His limbs were so weary that he would fain have gone straight to the inn and found supper and a soft bed; but he reflected that he must husband his money and find humbler quarters in some shed of hay. But first he had need of meat, so to the inn kitchen he went and ordered a modest meal, which he ate ravenously. The room was full of men talking hastily in a rich haze of tobacco smoke, and the stranger's entrance passed unnoticed. But Francis, weary as he was, could not keep from catching scraps of their conversation. In all a note of fear seemed dominant. Words – 'the Hielandmen,' 'Chairlie,' and a throng of ill-pronounced Gaelic names – occurred again and again till he was perforce roused to interest. Some great event must have happened since the morning, for the taking of Edinburgh was news already old. He touched the nearest speaker on the arm, and with his best politeness asked the cause of the uproar.

'Whaur d'ye come frae?' said the man, with the Lowland trick of answering with a new question.

'I'm frae the South,' said Francis, 'a weary traivel I have had. But I've heard no word of anything, so I beg ye to tell me.'

'Weel, it's just this. The lad they ca' the Prince has lickit

Johnnie Cope and the redcoats the day at Prestonpans, and the hale land is like to be fou o' skirlin' Hielandmen.'

Here was news. Francis' eye brightened, and he was for asking more. But the man had had enough of speaking to an ignorant stranger, and once more he was in the heat of debate, the subject apparently being an abstruse calculation of the time it would take this new power to give the country to the Pope.

'Sune,' said a grave old man, 'sune we'll see the fair eedifeece o' the Kirk coupit, and the whure o' Babylon, as ye micht say, up-haudin' her heid amang the ruins.'

'Sune,' said a Laodicean, 'we'll see something mair serious, a wheen men wi' red heids and naething on but sarks routin' ilka decent man out o' house and hame.'

Thereupon some eyes began to turn to Francis as the last comer and a probable centre of suspicion. His clothing marked him for higher quality than a countryman, and something ragged and desolate in his whole appearance might argue the Jacobite.

'What side are ye on, mannie?' one asked him.

'None. I am for my own hand,' said Francis truly, as he thought of his ill-fated incursion into high politics; and with a brief goodnight he rose to go.

The night had fallen with a great air of dew and freshness, and without in the village street the smoke smelled pleasantly in the nostrils, and the noise of the stream rose loud in the silence. From afar, as from the city, came an echo of a great stir, drums beating, maybe from the Castle, or pipers playing briskly over the victory. The sense of his desolation, his folly, the ruin of his hopes, smote heavily on Francis in this starry quiet. And with it all his weariness was so deep that it all but drowned the other; and finding a shed at the village end he lay down on a pillow of hay and was soon asleep.

He was wakened about nine in the morning by a heavy hand pulling at his coat. He stared sleepily and saw a man in the act of yoking a cart-horse, and another pulling his pillow from below his head. They were ready to abuse him for a gangrel, but something in his appearance as he rose stopped their tongues, and they gruffly assented as he gave them good morning and went out to the open. Half a mile farther on the road he bathed head and shoulders in a passing stream, and then, with some degree of freshness, set his face to the six-mile walk to the town. Again the day had risen fair, and all the way beneath the ancient trees or through fields of old pasture was fragrant with autumn scents. The electric air quickened him against his will, and he strode briskly along the curving highway till it dipped over a shoulder of hill to the city's edge.

That the place was in a ferment was clear from the din heard even at that distance – the intermittent note of bugles, the drone of pipes from different quarters, and at intervals the rattle of a drum. Francis found no guard set; in the great panic of the one party and the first jubilation of the other precautions had not yet entered men's minds. The cluster of little hamlets which lay around the city's extremities seemed quiet and deserted; doubtless all and sundry were even now adding their share to the main confusion. But when once he had entered the streets there was a different tale to tell. Never before had he seen the Highland dress on any number of men, and now the sight of bright tartans and fierce dark faces, as with a great air of triumph Macdonalds and Camerons hastened along the causeway, affected him with wonder. The honest burgesses wore woeful countenances, as they saw trade gone and gains lessened. The graver and more religious deplored the abomination at street corners in muffled tones for fear of the passing victors, while the younger sort, to whom the whole was a fine stage play, talked excitedly of the deeds of yesterday, the tales which rumour had already magnified. Francis heard names occur in the snatches of talk, names of Grants, Thrieplands, and Ogilvies, linked with stories of daring. The ferment was too high to admit of formalities, and each man joined the first group of strangers and bore his part in the frightened gossip. In this way he had the tale of the fleeing band of dragoons racing for the Castle with a single Highlandman at their heels, of the gate shut in his face and his defiant dirk stuck in the oaken panels. Confused tales of rank Hanoverian cowardice, the superhuman daring of the Prince's men, were diversified with wild speculating on the ultimate course of things. The Prince was already on his way to the capital, and in twelve hours the world would be turned topsy-turvy.

In all the stir Francis found himself in the position of a melancholy alien. He had no share in this triumph, no share even in the consolation of defeat. In all this babble of great deeds and brave men he must remain untouched, for had he not failed lamentably alike in loyalty and knavery? He was a mere popinjay, a broken reed, and to his unquiet sight there lurked a sneer in every passer's eye as if they divined his worthlessness. The man grew acutely miserable. This was his own city, his home; somewhere in this place his mother and sisters dwelt; the streets were sprinkled with his aforetime comrades. And he loathed them all: at the mere thought of his boyhood with its dreams of future bravado and its puerile vices, he sickened with disgust. Indeed this poor gentleman was fast approaching that attitude towards life which ends in its renouncement.

He drifted aimlessly to the end of the town where the streets were thronged to meet the coming army. The Camerons, who had marched straight from the battle, were there to meet them, and a host of great ladies and little lords with the Jacobite favours on their breasts and knots of white ribbon at bridle and sword-hilt. Even as he stood staring with lacklustre eyes at the sight, there rose through the lower gate the brisk music of the pipes and the tread of many men. No music has so dominant a note, and yet few are so adaptable. In the hour of death it rises and falls like the wail of a forlorn wind, at a feast it has the drunken gaiety of a Bacchante, and in the lost battle from it there comes the final coronach of vain endeavour. But in triumph it is supreme, a ringing call to action, a paean over the vanquished, the chant of the heroic. Now with its note went the tramp of feet and the chatter of horses' hooves, and then up the narrow street came the dusty, war-stained conquerors. A cry of welcome went up from God-fearing citizen and ragged

Jacobite alike, for in that moment creeds and practice were forgotten in the common homage to bravery.

But Francis had no eye for the lines of brown-faced men or the stained and ragged tartans. Among the bright crowd which greeted them were many whom he knew from old days, wits and gentlemen of the town, ladies of fashion, names linked with many tales. In some eyes shone the mere pleasure in a gallant show, some were wild with enthusiasm, some in a caustic humour. My Lord Cragforth kept up running comments with Mrs Cranstoun of Gair, and the young and witty Miss Menteith chattered to Lady Manorwater with a vivacity too sharp for enthusiasm. Young gentlemen with French elegance in their dress flicked the dust from their cravats, and smiled with gracious condescension to popular feeling. But others – rosy old lairds from the South and the dark retinue of Highland gentry – wore a different air. As the tune of 'The King shall enjoy his own again' – a catch long hummed in secret – rang clear and loud in the open street, their feelings rose beyond control, and with tears running down their cheeks those honest enthusiasts joined their prayers for the true King.

But with Lady Manorwater rode another, whom Francis' eyes followed till she was lost in the thickening crowd. She sat her grey horse and gazed on the advancing troops with eyes so honestly earnest, shining with such clear delight, that the throng on the causeway whispered her name with something like affection. Her bridle and trappings were decked with knots of white ribbon, and on her heart was pinned a cockade of white roses. The face above the dark velvet riding-cloak seemed pale with weariness – or was it excitement? – and her hand visibly trembled on the rein. The mark of her lash was still on Francis' cheek, but the sting on his soul smarted a thousandfold worse. Had she been gay and lively, he would have hated her like death, this woman who had mocked him. But her white face and the glory in her eyes affected him with a sentiment too elusive for words – a compound of pity and a hopeless emulation of a rare virtue.

He turned from the show down a little alley, and ran as if

from the avenger. Soon he came to more empty streets which the people had deserted for the sight of the entering army. He felt himself starving, so at a very little tavern he ordered a meal. But the food choked him, and he left the dish almost untasted.

He had no mind to think out a future course, for, at the present, emotion had broken down the last battlements of sober reason. Soon the street grew full again, and he had to bear the scrutiny of many eyes. He had no design in his walking; all he sought was to crush the hot pain of discomfiture which gnawed his heart. Once the coolest and most fearless, he grew as nervous as a woman. He fancied his life lay open like a book to every chance passer; he detected scorn in idly curious eyes. Sometimes he met a face he knew, but he waited for no recognition. His whole past life was so hateful to his thoughts that he shunned anything that might recall it. In his wanderings he passed by former haunts of his own, yea, under the very window of his mother's house. But old memories had no place in his mind; the dissolution of a scheme of life had crushed out the circumstances of his past. He had room merely for a bitter thought on the farce of this return to his native town; and then his mind was back once more in the dullness of regret.

Towards evening the stir died down, and save for the sight of armed men and the excited talk of street corners, he felt himself back in the Edinburgh of his youth. His misery only grew the more intolerable, but it seemed to shape to a purpose. He might yet redeem all and play a manful part in life. He had tried the role of the adventurer and failed; there yet remained the more difficult part of honour. The portrait of the lady which filled his mind seemed not wholly adamant. He had a dim remembrance of a gleam of pity at the inn, and the white light of enthusiasm at the pageant of the morning. He thought upon his first meeting at the House of Broughton, and her graciousness, which then had roused his bitterness, seemed now his one hope of salvation. Before, his pride had been his manliest attribute; now, he realized clearly and mournfully that the time had come to humble himself to virtue. It was a grievous thought to the arrogant nature, but as he wandered through the streets in the late afternoon he was compelled inexorably to submit. And as a purpose shaped itself his humility grew deeper, till it brought him to unconditional surrender.

In the High Street he asked of a Highlander the way to the lodging of Murray of Broughton. The man told him, adding that the Secretary was with the Prince at the Palace of Holyrood. The news gave him hope, and in the September dusk he found the house door with its watchful sentinel. Even now Francis' appearance was not discreditable: his clothes were good though sore worn, and he had just the figure that a poor loyalist would bear whose intentions were better than his fortunes. So the guard suffered him to pass, and the serving-man led him down a dark passage to a hall of some size and elegance. He was told that the Secretary's wife did much of her husband's work, often meeting the throng of visitors who crowded at all hours to the house. Now he was taken for one of those, and the servant opened a door and let him enter.

He found himself in a long dining-room wainscotted in brown oak, and lit by a blazing fire on the hearth. Two candles burned faintly on a table, where sat a lady poring over a great map. She started at his entrance, and then lifting a candle, came forward to scan his face. Meanwhile he was in a pitiable state of fear. He who had once been cool and self-possessed beyond the ordinary, now felt his knees sinking beneath him. Keenly and cruelly he felt the measure of his degradation, and the last rag of pride fell from the skeleton of his hopes.

She glanced at his face and stepped back. Wrath entered her eyes, to be straightway replaced by sheer perplexity. She looked again at the haggard figure before her, waiting for some word to explain his presence. But his tongue was tied, his speech halted and stammered, and he could only look with entreating eyes.

'And what is your errand, sir?' she asked. 'Has Lord Manorwater discharged you? I have not yet had time to tell him of your villainy, but doubtless he has found it out elsewhere.'

The words, with the sting of a lackey's reproach, were the needed stimulant to Francis' brain.

'I am no servant,' he said, and then hurriedly and brokenly he stammered a word of confession.

The lady drew back with angry eyes.

'And you dare to come to me and tell me this!' she cried. 'I had thought it was but greed and a servant's temptation, and now you cut off your own apology and confess yourself doubly a liar. Do you think to get anything for this penitence? Do you think that the Prince has open arms for all the rabble of the earth? Or do you wish to frighten a woman?' And she laid her hand on a pistol, and stood erect and angry like a tragedy queen.

'I seek nothing,' said Francis, with a groan. 'God knows I am not worth your thought.'

'You value yourself well, Mr What's-your-name? If I had known you as I know you now, no lash of mine would have touched you. A whipping is for a servant's fault, which may yet be forgiven. But for such as yours . . . Yet you are made in the likeness of a proper man,' and a note of wonder joined with her contempt.

The wretched Francis stood with bowed head beneath this tempest of scorn. The words fell on dulled ears. His own shame was too heavy on his mind to allow of a poignant feeling. He felt like some ineffectual knocker at a barred door, some vanquished invader trying to scale a hostile parapet. By his own folly he had fallen to a place forever apart from this proud woman's ken. He could but cry for pity like a child.

Then she cut short reproaches and looked at him keenly. Perhaps something in his face or his hopeless eyes struck a chord of pity. 'What may be your name?' she asked, 'if you say you are no servant.'

He told her shortly, though the words burned his lips.

'Birkenshaw!' she cried. 'Of the Yarrow Birkenshaws?' And then she fell to musing, looking up at him ever and again with curious eyes.

'I have heard the name. Maybe even it is kin to my own. I

have heard the name as that of a great and honourable house. And you have lived to defile it!' And for a little she was silent.

'I would to God,' she spoke again, 'that you had been Lord Manorwater's lackey.'

The man said nothing. Deep hidden in his nature was a pride of race and name, the stronger for its secrecy. Now he saw it dragged forth and used as the touchstone for his misdeeds. It was the sharpest weapon in the whole armoury of reproach. For one second he wished himself back in his old temper of mind. Why had he thus debased his manhood to the frigid and finicking virtue of a woman? Not till he looked again at the face of his inquisitor did he find justification for his course.

Again she spoke, but in an altered voice, and Francis seemed to read a hint of mercy.

'No,' she said, 'I was wrong. I am glad you are no lackey. Had you been but a lying servant there had been no room for repentance. But you come of honest folk, you have honest blood in your veins. Gentlemen are none so common that one should be lost in the making.' And she twined her fingers, deep in meditation, looking into the fire with a face from which all anger had departed.

Francis' clouded soul cleared at this dawn of hope. He watched the pale woman, and a sudden wild exaltation shook him. Sufficient, more than sufficient for him to do the bidding of this lady who had drawn him from the depths.

'Take me,' he cried. 'I am weak and foolish. I have no more sense than a bairn, and I have done the devil's work with an empty head. But I swear that this is bye and done with.'

'You have made ill work of it in the past, Mr Birkenshaw,' said the lady. 'Will you serve the Prince well, think you, if you have been false to me?'

'I can say naught,' said Francis, 'but I beseech you to give me trial.' And then with a touch of old bravado he added, 'I am a man who has seen much and can turn my hands and head to many purposes. I will prove myself worth the trusting.'

The lady frowned and tapped with her fingers on the table,

looking over his head to the wall beyond. 'You have much to learn,' she said gently. 'Do you think it is any merit in your services which would make me take you for the Prince?' Then, as if to herself, 'It is raw stuff, but it would be a Christian act to help in the shaping of it to honesty.'

Then with a sudden impulse she walked straight up to him and looked in his eyes. 'Lay your hand on mine,' she said, 'and swear. It is the old oath of my house, maybe, too, of your own. Swear to be true to your word, your God, and your King, to flee from no foe and hurt no friend. Swear by the eagle's path, the dew, and the King's soul.'

'I swear,' he said, his hand shaking like a leaf as it touched her slender wrist.

'Now you had better leave me,' she said. 'Maybe I have done wrong. I am but a weak woman, and the heart should be steeled for the high business which presses on the land. Yet you have sworn, and I have given you my trust. If you will come tomorrow morning you will learn my bidding.'

BOOK II

EIGHT

The Journey to the North

In the autumn dusk Mr Francis Birkenshaw rode down a path of mountain gravel into the glen of a little stream. Behind him were the flat meadows of his own country, with coiling waters and towns smoking in woody hollows. The sea lined the horizon with a gleam as of steel; and, fretted faintly against hillside and sky, all but vanishing into the evening haze, rose the spires of the town he had left. From the prosperous cornfields five miles back the way had risen slowly to the crest of a ridge, whence it turned sharply down to a cavernous mountain vale, which seemed to lead sheer into the heart of a gloomy land. All about were acres of dark hills, ribbed, curved, and channelled by myriad water-courses, forcing sharp peaks into the sunset or falling back in dismal lines to the east and north. Down the affronting cleft a storm was coming, and even as he looked it burst upon him, and he was cloaked in mist and rain.

He had ridden hard from Edinburgh since the previous morn with the speed of a zealous messenger. On the day before, when he had gone to the Murrays' lodging, he had been tried with many questions and then trusted with a message which even he, all untrained in the arts of war, knew to be of high import. His courage had half failed him: he had stammered modest excuses; and then, heartened by bright eyes and brave words, accepted his commission with diffident if resolute purpose. With a smile and a face in his memory he had ridden out on the morning of that day into the new world for him but two nights old. Never before had he felt such lightness of heart. The September sunrise had been a masque of purple and gold, the clear air a divine ether. Once more he had found a standing-ground from which to view the world; he could look frankly in each passer's eyes; and behind all was a woman's face in the gallery of his heart to comfort his travelling.

The thought of the complexity and peril of his mission was scarcely present. That was still in the far future. Meantime there was the fervour of hope recovered, a fervour still stung at intervals by flickers of old pride, and stronger still the half-pharisaic feeling which springs from a dawning virtue. He had no thoughts; the tumult of his feeling left no space for the clearer emotions. But the sense of wild adventure was strong upon him. He was venturing on an errand of war into a land as little known to him as the steppes of Tartary. And the eternal memory of the lady freshened his fancy till youth returned once more to the broken man who had two days before been at the feet of Fate. So with blithe heart he crossed the Firth by the Alloa ferry, where sea-breeze and land-breeze strive with the widening river, and took his path for the wall of mystic northern hills.

But now, as a darker country closed in on him, the strangeness began to weigh on his spirits. He was Lowland bred, and, with all his boasted experience, a traveller within but narrow limits. Moors he knew, the soft comely deserts which line Yarrow and Tweed and break ever into green vales and a land of meadows. But this was something new – this everlasting bleak land, where God's hand seemed to have placed no order. The stormy afternoon made the sight wilder, and all around him birds cried so constantly and so shrilly that the wilderness seemed to have taken to itself a voice. But soon his natural ardour rose triumphant to the influence of weather. All was but part of this new course, instinct with fierce adventure, a list for the conquest of haughty hearts. As the cold of evening grew, and heavy shadows fell on his path, he exulted in the mystery of his errand. He saw the long hillsides on either hand, grey with banks of rock and rough with birken tangles, down which at times came the cry of a fox or the croak of a raven. Little lochs were passed, framed in the ebony of black bogs or edged with dolorous rushes. All was strange, uncanny; and as he looked keenly for the light which would tell him of his journey's end and relief from the craggy path, he felt the joy of the crusader, the wanderer on a reputable errand.

But somewhere on the high hills a storm had gathered, and hurrying from mist-filled tarns choked the strait glens with sleet. It caught the traveller full in the face, and in a trice had him soaked to the bone. This was all that was needed to give the final exhilaration to his spirits. Gaily he urged his horse, wrapping his cloak about his shoulders and lowering his head to bide the brunt. It stung his face to fire, and sent the blood coursing through every vein. The man gloried in his strength. He cried defiance to all powers of weather, and thought lovingly on himself in this role of doughty knight-errant. Then through the sheer-falling water a light gleamed, all rayed like a star through the sleety veil; the way grew smoother; and Francis was aware of his lodging for the night.

Ere he had dismounted and stretched his legs, a throng of all ages and descriptions with lights of many sizes gathered about him. The place was small and the door narrow, and in contrast with the sharp out-of-doors the air smelled hot and close. Dazed like an owl, he stumbled down two steps into a wide, low room, where some dozen men sat drinking round the hearth or eating supper at a table. A fire of peat burned in the middle and the air was thick with a blue smoke, which gusts from a broken window were ever blowing aside. The inmates were all in Highland dress, save one man who was still at supper – a stout lantern-faced gentleman of middle age in knee breeches and a dark-blue coat. Room was made for Francis on the settle by his side, and a meal placed before him.

With keen appetite he fell to his supper, looking often and curiously at his companions. The place reeked of food and drink and generous living. In a corner stood a great anker of whisky with a spigot, whence the Highlanders replenished their glasses. A barrel of sugar with a small spade in it was by its side, and on the peats the water boiled for toddy. It was a good lodging for men who were fresh from wild, cold journeying, for such

had no mind to mark the filth which was everywhere, the slat-
ternly look of the maids, the exceeding dirtiness of the company.
The Highlanders were all tall men, with gaunt, dark faces and
ragged tartans. One of them, smaller in stature, wore the trews
instead of the kilt and seemed a thought more decent and
presentable. They talked rapidly among themselves in Gaelic,
and ever and again one would raise a catch, while the whole
motley crew would join in. It was with relief that Francis turned
from watching them to the comfortable figure at his side. He
caught the man's eye, and they gravely gave each other good
evening. Clearly he was a person of consequence, for his dress
was good, and his face had the tight lips and clean chin of one
used to give orders and be obeyed.

'It's a coarse day for a journey, sir,' said he. 'Ye'll be going
south to Edinburgh?'

'Even so,' said Francis, 'and I hope to have the pleasure of
your convoy on the road tomorrow.' This personage had the
look of a Whig, and there was no need to enlighten him.

'I am at your service,' said the elder man, with a twinkling
eye. Francis caught the twinkle and put a stricter bridle upon
his tongue.

'I hear,' said he again, 'that there are stirring times in
Edinburgh. We country folk in the North hear nocht of a thing
till it's bye.'

Francis saw the guile and checked the natural desire of the well-
informed to make a present of his knowledge to every inquirer.
'I've heard something like it,' he said, 'but we'll not be long in
hearing the truth. How far is it maybe from here to the town?'

The other's cheeks grew red with suppressed amusement.
'That was the very question I was on the point of asking you
myself,' he said. 'But go on with your supper, sir, and do not let
me hinder a hungry man.'

Francis ate with sidelong glances at his companion, who had
lit a pipe and smoked vigorously. Once and again he met his eyes,
and both smiled. This game of hide and seek was becoming
amusing. Then he fell to studying the image of the man's looks as

pictured in memory. Some hint of a likeness struck him; these lineaments, that figure were known to him. Carefully he traced the web of his recollections, but could find no thread. Doubtless he had seen him in the old Edinburgh days, but where? when? He had all but finished his meal when a sudden lift of his comrade's arm, a motion to set right his cravat, furnished the key to the mystery. He had mind of days in the Parliament House, when he, the lawyer's clerk, took notes and papers to the great lawyers. Softly he whistled to himself, blinking with amazement. The Lord President! So far, so good; he had the advantage of his companion; doubtless the famous Mr Duncan Forbes had no wish to be recognized in this Highland tavern.

'It's a wild night,' said Francis. 'Had ye a hard day's riding?'

'Dub and mire,' said the other. 'Ye're splashed yourself, so ye ken the state of the roads.'

'I think I had a glisk of ye five mile back at the bridge end,' hazarded the bold Francis.

'Maybe so. I had a mettle beast, and took the road well.'

'Ay,' said Francis meditatively, 'it's a lang dreary road to Culloden,' and he looked innocently at his neighbour.

The man raised his eyebrows a trifle and bowed. 'It appears,' he said, 'that my name and designation are better kenned in the land than I had thought. Ye have the advantage of me, Mr –'

'Robertson,' said the other, 'Mr George Robertson, merchant in the Pleasaunce of Edinburgh, returning from transacting some business in the North.'

Francis had overshot himself, and the man smiled. 'I am at your service, Mr Robertson of the Pleasaunce. Your name and trade do credit to your honesty and your own pretty fancy,' and with a sly glance he knocked the ashes from his pipe.

The ground was dangerous, and Francis sheered away. Moreover, the rest of the company were fast approaching the state of maudlin good-fellowship which follows the pugnacious. The smell of hot drink was grateful in his nostrils after the bitter wind, and he was in a cheerful mood at the discomfiture of his neighbour. He filled a great jug with the piping stuff, and drank

deeply to some chance toast. The liquor was raw and fiery, and it
sensibly quickened his vivacity. Memories came back of old
tavern nights in his boyhood. The smell of the place, the uproari-
ous company fostered the impression, and for a little rough
hilarity seemed the extreme of joy. The man's mind was elated
by the day's ride, and still more by the sudden rebound from
black despair. His animal boisterousness, always at hand in his
nature, was beginning to assert itself under the influence of
keen air and this northern whisky. He filled Mr Forbes' glass till
the gentleman cried a truce, and toasted him with clinking
bowls. Then he grew friendly with the others at the table. The
little man in the trews made the first overtures to friendship by
coming over to the pair, bowing with profound if drunken
gravity, and asking them for their commands. Francis received
him as a brother, and ere he knew, found himself singing riot-
ously among the ragged Highlanders. Toasts in Gaelic were
drunk with such generous frequency that Mr Francis Birkenshaw,
who had not been drunk above three times in his previous life,
who had only that morn been a very storehouse of high sentiments, who was even now pluming himself on a diplomatist's
wisdom, became gloriously overcome.

It is the nemesis of a vagrant youth that when at a later time
the keynote is struck of some one of its youthful follies the
maturer nature instinctively responds. The mere flavour of
good-fellowship had brought him to a condition of which he
would have been heartily ashamed even in his earliest lawlessness. Once more he was the vicious boy; his tongue was loosed,
and he drew from the rich storehouse of his former experience.
Soon the wild talk of the company had been raised to a pitch of
indecent blasphemy which before it had wholly failed to attain;
and the Highlanders, imperfect as was their English, looked
with awe and reverence on this young spirit whose speech was
even as the common sewer. Gaelic and English alternating filled
the place with a din like Bedlam, while ever and anon some
loyalist sentiment gave a chance for maudlin tears.

In a sudden spasm of such feeling the company waxed political.

'Drink, gentlemen,' cried Francis, 'to the only King, the only Prince, and the only Cause. Drink good luck to all honest fellows who take their sword in their hand and their plaid on their back when their master bids them. May the dirty German be sent packing and our ain lad sit in St James's.'

All rose with wild cries and breaking glass, and a shrill Gaelic song, wild as a gled's scream, rasped through the place. All save one – the sober Mr Forbes, who sat smiling and self-possessed in his chimney-corner.

Then arose Long John of the Dow Glen with his broken speech. 'There iss a man, a fat Southron of a man, who will not trink to the goot causs. By Heaven, he will get something mair in hiss guts than usquebagh, if he toes not.' Robin Mactavish and Hamish the Black added like comments. The little man with the trews was too far gone to speak, but he waved a threatening glass.

Francis had still the wits to refrain from shouting the dissenter's name. But he called on him to drink to the King, or he, Mr Francis Birkenshaw, would know the reason.

'I will drink a toast, Mr Robertson (or is it Mr Birkenshaw?),' said the man, and he rose slowly to his feet. 'Gentlemen all,' he cried, 'I drink – to all good intentions.'

The words sounded satisfactory and a great shout was the reply, as each man interpreted the toast into the tongue of his own sentiments.

But Francis was little content. 'Ye're a Whig,' he cried, 'a smooth-spoken whigamore, unfit for the company of honest gentlemen.' And he turned on him with the abuse of the stableyard.

For a second the two were left alone, for a debate had arisen between Robin the Piper and him of the Dow Glen, which distracted the others. The older man looked at his drunken opponent with angry and pitiful eyes.

'Your speech, sir,' he said, 'is most filthy and shameful. You belong to the wrong side, and I am glad of it, for it would be a disgrace for the right party to have you. But you have women in your cause whose memory should bridle your tongue. I know

naught of you or your business, but it little becomes a man thus
to forget himself, when he is of the same persuasion as so many
honest ladies.'

'You have spoken the word, sir,' said Francis. 'And now I
propose that you join me in drinking to the best and bonniest.
Gentlemen,' he cried, 'I give you the toast of the bonny Mrs
Murray.'

The whole tipsy company caught at the name and drank deep
to the health of the famous lady, some calling her by her strange
Gaelic name, which meant 'the dew of April'. In the wildest
glens of the North the story was told of her beauty, and she was
as often on loyal lips as the Prince himself. So with all the
goodwill in the world the tipsy crew cried her name, while Mr
Forbes sat gloomily and angrily silent.

Francis awoke the next morning with a burning head and a
heart from which all gaiety had gone. He dressed with woebe-
gone leisure and came into the kitchen rubbing weary eyes. The
place was quiet utterly; about the door hens were clucking, a great
hum of the farmyard was in the air, and through the open
entrance he saw the high steep shoulder of a hill. The company
of the night before had gone early; in some haste he looked about
for the Lord President, but he too had departed. He went out of
doors and smelt the fresh air of morn. The rain had gone, and the
narrow vale was bright with sun and swollen water. But the sky
warned him that he had slept late, so he cried for the hostess. She
came, wiping her hands, a miracle of dirty unkemptness. 'Where
had the others gone?' he asked. 'Ach, their own ways.' 'She kent
nocht of the folk that cam to her public.' She was 'only a poor
woman fightin' to keep body and saul together in evil days. All
had left early, even the old man that was sae brawly drest.' Francis
plied her with irritable questions on the way he had taken. But
the woman was trusty; Whig or Jacobite were naught to her, she
would tell nothing of her guests; and to aid her pious resolution
she discovered opportunely that she knew no more English than
the barest smattering.

So he must needs take things as he found them, breakfast on

eggs, pay a modest lawing, and ride off in a violent ill humour. The memory of the night's doings rankled in his heart. He had forfeited all claim to that character to which he fairly thought he had attained. He had slipped back to the worst days of his youth, and got drunk in the company of filthy barbarians. The figure of the Lord President added bitterness to his reflections. The man of the world, the true man of affairs, had despised him as a lecherous boy. He pictured his own tipsy abandonment, his talk, his maudlin jests, all watched with the keen eyes of the greatest man in the country. The shame of the thing made him cry out and curse his fortune.

But the gall of the matter was his toasting of his mistress. In his sober hours the very speaking of her name in such a company and such a place seemed the sheerest blasphemy. And the circumstances of the toast, the drunken laughter, the foul talk, the brazen defiance of all decency, made the crime more heinous. In a common alehouse he had insulted, grossly insulted, the name of her who had given him a reason to live.

He reviewed every scene in his drama where she had entered – the midnight raid on the House of Broughton, the tragic farce at the inn, the sight of the lady on the grey horse in the street of Edinburgh, and finally that strange meeting in her own house where he had seen the full nakedness of his soul. The memory of her face nigh drove him frantic. He was riding on her errand, and lo! he had betrayed her at the very outset.

But with the progress of the day his mind grew quieter. The more poignant shame died down, leaving only a regret. The weather was clear and bright, autumn without storm and heaviness. The road rose slowly from the straiter glens to a high tableland, where shallow vales marked the extreme waters of young rivers. A wide country lay bare to the view, all alike rough with wood and heather; while in the distance a circle of dark mountains made a barrier as of some great amphitheatre.

The place had a soothing effect upon his spirits. Something in the moorland peace, the quiet of these endless fields of heather where deer couched and wild birds nested, brought ease and some sanity of mind. To the man who knew only the city wynds and the shrill-sounding beaches of Fife, this untilled land had an exquisite and elemental freshness, as of the primeval world.

At a turn in the road he saw a rider before him not a quarter of a mile ahead. He drew back and stared. Something in the figure and carriage were familiar. The man was riding in a hurry, for he used his whip frequently and with vigour. Then recollection came to Francis, and in spite of his gloom he had almost laughed.

This was indeed the Lord President Forbes on his way to his house of Culloden, doubtless on some sudden business of state. The man's composure was almost restored. Clearly the great statesman feared him; he had been at the pains to deceive him and rise early to outwit him. Strange are the crannies of our nature; for it is a fact that the sight lessened Francis' self-loathing and the bitterness of Mr Forbes' reproof. After all, he was still of some consequence in the world, and though his heart was repentant it was remorse without pain.

NINE

My Lord of Lovat

That night he lay at a wretched cottage by the wayside where the hill air came through the gaps in the heather roof and made the sleeper shiver on his couch of grass. The land was now a mere chaos of black mountains, and the road, which at first had borne some likeness to a highway, was now sunk to an ill-marked scar through the moss.

It made heavy riding, and through the next day our traveller felt more weary than he cared to own. Had not the sun been bright and the weather dry, he might have missed the track utterly, for the bogs which lay among the hills were hard to wrestle through. At evening he was fain to stop at a hut which lay on the side of a long hill called Corryarrick, up which the road went in corkscrew fashion for half a score of miles. The man of the place gave him some kind of oaten porridge and a raw whisky which burned his palate, and told him many details of his way. This, it appeared, was still the country of the Atholl Stewarts, but over the affronting hills began the lands of Stratherick and the domain of the Frasers. The fellow had little good to say of them; nay, by his account they were a clan of gruesome savages hated of God and their neighbours. So it was with some foreboding that Francis at the next dawning set his horse's face to the ascent.

All that day he rode in a bleak land, where wild tracts of moss with shining lochs scattered athwart them were frowned on by murky hills. And, to make the road worse, the place was scarred with horrific ravines running to the westward, at whose bottom foamed impetuous rivers. At the best they were spanned by rough bridges of tree trunks and heather, but more than once there was nothing for it but to make the steep descent and breast the waters. The day was still cloudless, but what with many wettings and the hardships of the path Francis fell into a dismal frame of mind. No human dwelling relieved the inhospitable waste, his store of provisions failed, and, to crown all, his horse fell lame at the crossing of a burn and had to be led heavily through the hags.

In the late afternoon three men arose as if from the bowels of the earth, and laid hands on horse and man. As it chanced, this was the best thing that could have happened, for they were men of Lovat's own clan in Stratherick, filthy, thieving rascals, but loyal to their lord. So it fell out that when they had plied Francis with unintelligible Gaelic, one, more learned than the rest, asked his name and business in a travesty of English. He replied that he sought the house of Macshimei at Castle Dounie, for so he had been told to speak of the head of the clan. The bare word was enough for the men, who straightway became friendly and set to relieve his wants. They dressed his horse's knee with a concoction of herbs, bandaging it after a fashion of their own, and led Francis to a cluster of cabins on the edge of a long loch. Here they gave him meat – roast moorfowl and eggs and oatcake, with a glass of excellent brandy. And in the morning one undertook to guide him past the narrows of the loch and set him well on his way to his destination.

When in the afternoon he crossed the river which formed the outlet of the lake, he found himself on the confines of a pleasant country. Set like an oasis among the stormy deserts lay meadows and haughlands and a fringe of woods, while beyond gleamed a quiet stretch of sea. The place was green and habitable, and on Francis' wearied eyes it fell like a glimpse of an Arcady. He could scarce believe his senses, for this looked more like the Lothians or the cornlands of Fife. But the high brown towers of the castle rising from the seaward slope and the bald scarp of Lovat on a cape in the Firth told of a chieftain's dwelling. The sky was darkening towards evening as he rode to the great pile, and his heart again misgave him. He was on a nicely diplomatic errand, one, too, not without its peril. The man who dwelt there was one of the most famous names in the land, ill-reputed for lawlessness and treachery, notorious for a wit too subtle for prosaic earth. Who was he, a raw, unlettered vagrant, to meet such a one face to face and teach him his business? He was tired to death, too, with his moorland journey, and his brain was half-clouded with sleep.

There was no guard at the gate – nothing save two unkempt serving-men quarrelling over a jug of ale. They asked his business with a high gravity and led him into a damp courtyard where children squalled and serving-women chattered.

The informality of such a place restored Francis to self-confidence, and he followed his guides with an assured step. A noise of rackety mirth fell on his ear, and he was ushered into the dining-hall of the castle, where some fifty and more men sat at meat. The air was thick with the fumes of wine and hot dishes, barefooted gillies ran hither and thither, and it took no extraordinarily acute eye or nostril to perceive that the place was exceeding dirty. At the lower end of the great table a crowd of ragged and dishevelled men quarrelled and scrambled for bones and offal. Thence there seemed to rise degrees of respectability from the common herd who supped on sheep-heads and whisky to the more honoured, the lesser gentry of the clan, who had good beef and mutton and plenty of claret. At the very top sat the lord himself with his more distinguished friends, Frasers of Gortuleg, Phopachy, and Byerfield, eating French dishes and drinking choice wines. One of the ragged servants went to the chief's ear and whispered as he had been bidden, 'Mr Francis Birkenshaw with a message from Mr Murray of Broughton'; and straightway room was made for the traveller at the honourable end of the table.

The cooking was of the finest, and Francis appeased his hunger with great satisfaction. No notice of him was taken by his neighbours to left and right, but each listened to my lord's pleasantries with the anxious care of the retainer. From the great man himself Francis could not keep his eyes, and in the pauses of the meal he found himself narrowly watching the mighty figure lolling in his carven armchair. Already beyond the confines of old age, an ungainly form with legs swollen with the gout and a huge rolling paunch, he lay in his seat like a mere drunken glutton. But when the eye passed from his body to the ponderous face and head, the mind drew his nature in different colours. The brow was broad and wrinkled with a thousand lines, hanging heavy over his eyes and fringed with great grey eyebrows. The thick fleshy nose, the coarse lips, the flaccid grey cheeks, were all cast in lines of massive strength, and the jaw below the cunning mouth was hard as if cut in stone. But the most notable point in the man was the pair of little eyes, still keen as a ferret's, and cruel in their resolute blue. He ate ravenously, and drank scandalously of every wine, keeping all the while a fire of compliments and jocularities, coarse as the gutter, at which the obedient assembly roared.

By and by, and not for a good hour, the feast came to an end, and the old lord was lifted from his seat by two servants. 'Gentlemen,' he cried, 'there will be supper here in a matter of two hours, beefsteaks and claret for all that wish them. See that no man goes empty out of this house of Dounie. For mysel', ye see that the infirmities of age creep over me, and the thrang o' many cares compels me to quit ye. Guid e'en to ye, friends, guid fare and a safe returning.' And he hobbled away, leaning heavily on his bearers.

After his departure the table was turned into a scene of riot, all shouting in Gaelic, drinking queer toasts and quarrelling at times in pairs and threes. Francis felt sadly out of place in a company where he was known to none and heard nothing but a strange language. So when a gillie touched his sleeve and bade him follow, for 'Macshimei wad speak with him,' he rose gladly and left the reeking hall. The man led him into another room furnished with some approach to comfort, where rugs of deerskin covered the nakedness of the stone floor; thence into a passage which led to a narrow stone stair; and finally stopped at the entrance of a little turret-room. With an air of deep secrecy he tapped twice, and then with a flourish opened the door and showed Francis in, crying the announcement, 'To speak with ta Lord Lovat.'

The place was little and bright, with a cheerful fire and a long couch of skins. So thick were the walls, so narrow the space, that Francis felt himself secluded from the world. The chief lay stretched out with his feet to the blaze, a little black table with wine at his elbow. He looked up sharply at the entrance, and then stared once more into the fire as Francis came forward and stood before him.

After a little he raised his head. 'Young man,' he said, 'I pray you sit down. See to your ain comfort. Ye are admitted to a private and secret audience with a man who is not accessible to all. I trust ye have the sense to value your preevilege.'

Francis bowed in some confusion. The look of arrogant strength in this strange old man crushed his spirits. He sorely distrusted his own wits in contest with this rock of iron.

'Ye will have a letter from the Secretary?'

'Indeed, no,' said Francis, 'for the matter is somewhat too long for a letter. It is a thing for a discussion, my lord, and not for a scrawl on paper.'

The old man looked grimly at the speaker. 'And who are you, in God's name,' he rasped out, 'that is thocht worthy to come and treat wi' me? – me, the first lord in the Hielands, the friend o' princes.'

'My name is Francis Birkenshaw, at your service,' said the other, conscious that those shrewd eyes were scanning every line in his face, every thread in his garments.

Once more his catechist plied him. 'Are ye gentrice?' he asked.

At this some heat came into Francis' blood, and he answered warmly, 'I am even as yourself, my lord. My descent is none so regular, but I have the name and blood of a gentleman.'

Lovat frowned crossly, for the scandals of his family were common talk. 'Ye have a ready tongue in your head, sir, but ye are somewhat lacking in respect. So ye are one of Murray's packmen?'

He waited for an answer but Francis held his peace. 'Ay,' he went on, 'a deeficult, dangerous job. Murray's a shilpit body, a keen man for his ain guid, but without muckle penetration. But his wife – weel, d'ye ken his wife?'

'I have the honour of her acquaintance,' said Francis stiffly.

'Have ye indeed?' said Lovat, smiling. 'A fine woman, then, I can tell ye, sir. A bonny bitch! A speerity licht sort o' body!' and he looked from below his eyebrows to see the effect of his words.

'If you will pardon me, sir,' said Francis, 'I fail to see your point. You are talking of the character of those with whom I have nothing to do. Be assured I did not ride over your wet hills to indulge in moral disquisitions.'

The man laughed long to himself. 'So that's your talk,' he said, 'and you're no one o' Murray's fighting-cocks? Weel, the better for my business. Help yoursel' to some wine, Mr Birkenshaw, for it's drouthy work talking.'

Further, he bade Francis draw his chair nearer the fire and stir the logs to a blaze. Then silence reigned in the room, while the elder man stared into the glow with a face which even in the dim light seemed to his companion to be working with some emotion.

'It's a queer warld,' he said at length, 'and for the auld a cruel one. Be sure, Mr Birkenshaw, that it is a painful thing to feel the life sinking in your members and to mind again and again o' the days when ye were young and bauld. "*Eheu fugaces labuntur anni*". Weel, weel, it's the destiny of all.'

He lay back on his couch so mighty a wreck of a man that Francis' pity was stirred. He was himself of just such a spirit, and he could forecast in imagination the bitter ebbing of vital force. He nodded gravely to each sentence. Then the old lord spoke again with a sharper tone.

'Ay, but that is no the worst of an auld man's lot. Ye see me here, me that has been the peer o' the best in the land, forced to keep the company o' a wheen wild caterans, and all the while the country asteer wi' war. I am auld and puir and weak, and so I maun sit still in this lonely stane tower and hear o' great events through the clash o' packmen. Once,' and his voice rose high and querulous, 'once I was the great Lord Lovat, and every man was cap in hand as I came down the High Street o' Edinburgh. Mair, far mair – I hae carried the King himsel', God bless him, in my arms through the gardens o' Kensington, and my word was maybe no the least noted in his councils. There have been days, sir, when I walked in St James's Park, and many a braw lady cast eyes on the chief o' the Frasers and many great lords were proud to deck my arm. And now I maun dwine away my life in the midst o' cauld hills and heathery mosses. I have no complaint against a merciful God, but is it not a sair dispensation? But were this all, I would say ne'er a word. But in my day I have had the feelings, ay, and maybe done the work, a states-man and a patriot. I have sat at the council board with Hamilton and Queensberry, I have been the trusted adviser of Buccleuch and Tweeddale and Aberdeen, and not once or twice, but a score o' times, did Maccallum Mhor himself call me his friend. Can I sit still then and see the land divided against itself, one king on the throne and another in the heather, and the wisest heads in braid Scotland at desperation wi' loyalty and religion pulling one way and common prudence the ither? Ay, and I maun sit and see and groan in my inmost heart, and all the while be sae clogged wi' this perishin' body that I canna move.'

Lovat spoke fiercely and quickly. Francis was dimly conscious of the grandiloquence, but the strength of the recumbent figure made it seem only fitting.

'And then,' the old man continued, 'there is a different side to the whole matter. Now in this, the hinner end o' my days, I am quit o' all personal ambition, but I canna help that natural pride which the chief must feel in his own people. All the great north-ern clans are taking sides – Macdonalds, Camerons, and Stewarts for the Prince; Macleods and Mackays against him. And whatever way it falls out they will aye have taken their part in the battle and won great glory. Is it like,' he said simply, 'that I could endure that the Frasers should lie quiet like auld wives or young bairns? You will pardon my enthusiasm for a poor, rude, ignorant people, but they have followed me and my fathers and love my house dearly.

Nay, sir, you who ken but the folk of the towns and the south country can have little notion of these poor folk's loyalty. I am called the thirty-eighth of my name, and for every Lord of Lovat they have spilled their blood like water. But now in the evil days, when their lands are narrowed, and men who ken nothing but how to fight must set themselves to tillage, you can believe that their heart is cast down. They look to me to help them, and I have nothing to give them, so the poor folk must quit their bits o' shielings and the kindly glens where their fathers have dwelt since first a Frisel set foot in Scotland, and gang east and west and south to ither lands and stranger peoples. And there they make what shift they can to live, but their hearts are aye sair for the heathery hills and the auld glens and waters. I am no a man easily moved to tears, but the thought of my poor folk makes me greet like a bairn.'

The melancholy voice, the sorrowful words, and the great figure, which, seen in the dim light, had lost all coarseness and was only majestic, thrilled Francis in spite of himself. He had come with a distrust of this man, with a mind well stored with tales of his extraordinary character, and in consequence he had brought to the meeting a heart triply bound against emotion. But this air of lingering pity was overcoming him. This fusion of the complaint of an exiled Aristides with the lament of a chief over the past glories of his clan was affecting in the extreme.

Then the other changed his tone utterly. Raising himself from his couch, he looked over to Francis with a keen face of interrogation. 'I ken naught of your politics, Mr Birkenshaw, though from your errand I might make a guess. But I assume that ye are an honest, open-minded man, and I will do ye the honour to speak plainly. I live out o' the warld, but I have een in my head to see. We will leave the question of politics aside, if you please, for the moment. It may be that I am for the present king, it may be for him that's ower the water. But, at any rate, the blood o' my fathers in my veins still cries out to strike a blow for a Stuart, and I canna see the Cause misguided without a pang. And what is it that I see? A brave young lad wi' nae experience o' war and little

knowledge o' men, and a' around him a cleckin' o' wild Highland
chiefs who fecht for their ain hand and nothing besides. And
them that micht be advisers, what are they? A wheen bairnly
boys, wi' guid coats on their backs and fine names, very ready wi'
their bit swords, but poor silly sheep in the day of battle. Take my
word, Mr Birkenshaw, there are only two heads in the hale
concern. There's the Atholl Murray, Lord George. I bear nae guid
will to him, but at least he is a man and a soldier. And there's
Murray o' Brochtoun. Weel, the less said o' him the better. I have
come across him in mony a ploy, and the heart o' him is as rotten
as peat. But he is a man o' pairts, his hand is in the making o'
every plan, and abune a' he has his bonny wife to help him. It's
kenned that she has a' her lovers at her back, and that means
half the gentry o' the land.'

The old man leaned forward and scanned Francis' face. It was
his aim to find out how far this messenger was sent by a petti-
coat, and to set him against his mistress. He had chosen his
words with exquisite cunning, and he awaited the effect. Nor
was he disappointed. The young man's face, to his own huge
irritation, flushed deeply, and he seemed suddenly bereft of
words. His reason told him that such confusion was unwarrant-
able; it was no news to him that Mrs Murray, the admired of all,
had a train of gallants at her bidding. But the fact had never
appeared to him so real; he had felt, he knew not why, that in this
woman he had a private interest; his goddess seemed tarnished
by a hint of common worship. Lovat's plan had been well calculated, but he had just missed by a hair the proper estimate of his
companion's character. Instead of the irritation with the world
and despair which such news would have roused in the common
man of sentiment, in Francis it merely awakened a deeper
humility, a keener feeling of his own insignificance, a more
hopeless devotion. The thought that his sentiment was shared
by many showed the vast distance which separated her high
virtue from his folly. Somehow the shaft had not only missed its
mark, but performed the very work which its sender dreaded.

'I have spoken to you as friend to friend, Mr Francis Birkenshaw,' said Lovat. 'Ye see my unhappy position. An alien to those in authority, prevented by my weakness from vigorous action, I must decide one way or another for my clan. Ye see the responsibility and the hardship.'

Francis muttered assent, but his wits were busy with another question – whither all this talk was tending. He had his clear mission to win this lord to the Prince's cause, but the problem had now a different aspect. With much trepidation he waited on the issue of affairs.

But Lovat had little disposition to give a ready answer. 'Have ye any news for my ear?' he asked. 'I have heard of the victory at Prestonpans, but I would like to ken if any mair lords have risen, if England is yet ripe, and if the army has gotten an increase.'

Francis could say nothing but that Lord Lovat appeared as well informed as himself.

'Tut, tut, but this is a difficult business,' said the old man, and he stared once more into the fire. 'See here, sir, you see the wretched way I am placed. God knows I hold my country's welfare next to my own soul. I am ower auld to care a straw about which king has his backside on the throne; all I seek is that the land prosper. But it seems to me that the scales are about level. James would make a good king, and there's nae doubt but he has the richt on his side. Geordie makes a tolerable show, and if Chairlie is no strong enough to ding Geordie down, why, there Geordie will sit. If I thocht that there was a fair chance, I would set a' my people off the morn to fecht for the Stuarts. If I was clearly persuaded that there was none, they would join the ither side with all dispatch, that the rising might be the sooner quelled and peace restored. I am ower auld to take the field mysel', and it's for my poor feckless folk I maun consult. But the devil of it is that I canna make up my mind one way or anither. I live ower far out o' the warld, and I've ower little news. My friends among the Jacobites are wi' the Prince, my friends on the ither side, like the Lord President, are a' in Edinburgh and like to be there for mony a day. Truth, I kenna where to turn,' and he looked to the other with an air of great perplexity.

'On one matter I can ease your mind,' said Francis. 'I overtook the Lord President on the road, and as he was some three hours before me, he will be at his house of Culloden ere now.'

Lovat shot one sharp glance at the speaker. 'Say ye sae,' said he. 'Weel, I'm glad of it. But I fear ye maun be wrong, for Duncan in a time like this would come first to Castle Dounie. It was aye his way wi' his auld friends.'

At the words and the look which accompanied them, Francis had some suspicion that the presence of the Lord President in the North was well enough known to his interlocutor. He declared bluntly that he knew the face and had made no mistake.

'Weel, weel, we'll let the matter be,' said Lovat. 'If ye're richt, sae muckle the better for me. But how can I make up my mind when I get such word as this?' and he reached his hand to a packet of papers. 'Here is a memorandum from Culloden's self with great news o' King George's forces and the peaceable and law-abiding spirit of the citizens of Edinburgh and the folk of the South. "My dear lord," he says, "I do assure you that the thing will be nipped in the bud, so I counsel you to take no rash steps." So says Mr Duncan; but what says Lochiel? "All the land is with us; forbye there are ten thousand French to be landed immediately, while in England every house of distinction is all for us and our Prince." God, Mr Birkenshaw, if ye had brought news to settle this kittle point, ye would have been an acceptable messenger.'

Francis was in a quandary from which he saw no outlet. This man was clearly playing high for his own hand, but he had cloaked it cunningly under a pretence of love of clan and country. So he spoke guardedly. 'You make the question difficult, my lord; but if the odds are so even, if whatever way you turn a like peril attends you, is there no sentiment to turn the scales?'

Lovat nodded wisely. 'There ye are right,' he said. 'I have a sentiment for the old house, which is ever tugging against my prudence. When I heard the news o' Prestonpans I was daft. I cast my hat on the ground and drank damnation to the White Horse o' Hanover, and this very day I had seven hundred men drilled on the green, a' wi' their white cockades and sprigs o' yew in their bonnets. Were I no a discreet and well-principled man, the clan would ere now have been marching over Corryarrick.'

Francis spoke with rising irritation. 'You see that I can advise you nothing, my lord. My opinion on the enterprise is my own, but I am here with a clear message. Are you willing to take a step and trust your fortunes and your clan's to God and the Prince, or will I take back the answer that my Lord Lovat is old and timid and prefers to bide at home?'

'Na, you will do no siccan thing. I was but talking the matter over in a' its bearings, for my mind was made up lang syne. I am faun in years, but my spirit is not quenched, and it will never be said that the chief o' the Frasers was feared to take a chance. But I am no young hot-head to rin at the sound of a trumpet, and my habit of due consideration is strong in all things. Just rax me that pen, Mr Birkenshaw, and I will write the Secretary the word ye want.'

The old lord mended a quill and wrote diligently for some minutes, while Francis watched the great mask-like face with a mixture of admiration and distrust. He dimly guessed at the purpose of the whole talk, and this sudden decision did not increase his faith. By and by the writer finished and looked up with a twinkling eye. 'Ye're a trusted servant of the Cause, Mr Birkenshaw, so ye'll be preevileged to hear a bit o' my epistle. Am I to add any kind messages about yoursel'? Ye will see that I have omitted no one of the flowers o' sentiment which ye so admire.' And he read:

'I solemnly protest, dear sir, that it was the greatest grief of my life that my indisposition and severe sickness kept me from going south to my dear brave Prince, and never parting with him while I was able to stand, but venture my old bones with pleasure in his service and before his eyes, while I had the last breath within me. But I send my eldest son, the hopes of my family and the darling of my life, a youth about nineteen years old, who was just going abroad to finish his education, after having learned with applause what is taught in our Scots universities, and was graduate Master of Arts. But instead of sending him abroad to complete his education, I have sent him to venture the last drop of his blood in the glorious Prince's service; and as he is extremely beloved, and the darling of the clan, all the gentlemen of my name (which, I thank God, are numerous and look well and are always believed to be as stout as their neighbours) are gone with him.'

'What do ye think o' that effort in your own line, sir?'

'I am not sure that I take your meaning,' said Francis. 'You cannot go yourself, but you will send the clan under your son?'

'That is my meaning,' said Lovat, 'and what do you think of it?'

'Why, that it is most honourable and generous,' said Francis, in incredulous tones.

The old lord looked at him for a little, then pursed up his mouth and smiled. 'Honour and generosity,' he said, 'are qualities o' my house, and we'll let that subject alane. But I look to reap the reward o' my action, sir. This is no wild clanjamphray sent down from the hills, but a great and weel-disciplined clan, wi' my own son at its head. If the rising ends in naething, then there's my poor folk at the mercy o' their enemies, when they were sent out maybe against their will by their chief, who a' the while was well disposed to both governments. If, again, the Prince gets his desires, there is honour and glory for man and master. I put both possibilities before you as a man o' some sense and experience, and I trust that if the first case come about before ye get the length o' the Prince's army, this letter whilk I have written will never get farther than your pocket. And further, that supposing you have delivered it, you will do your best to see it destroyed.'

Francis stared in downright amazement. This was an extreme of brazen audacity which he had not reckoned with. The man's eyes were peering into his, and every line of that strange face spoke of daring and wit. 'But,' he stammered, 'the clan will be out, and that will involve you without any scrawl of writing.'

'Preceesely,' said Lovat, 'the clan will be out, but perhaps it may be in spite o' their loyal chief, who sits at hame lamenting their defection and the woeful ingratitude of children.' His face was filled with sardonic mirth as he watched the changing features of his companion.

But Francis was already roused to keen suspicion, and he found at once voice and a cool bearing.

'Your methods are simple, my lord, and do credit to your politic mind. I will not say that they are dishonourable, for I have no reason to judge you. You have talked to me of your forethought for your people, which does you credit, and if this were the only motive your policy might be blameless. But I have heard talk of a dukedom for the lord of Lovat if all turned out well.'

'Ay, and what of that?' asked the old man, with great calmness.

'Why, this,' said Francis, 'that if a man have recourse to tricks for the sake of others, he is pardoned, but if for his own advantage, he gets a more doubtful name.'

'Meaning?' said the other.

'Meaning,' said Francis, 'that men use the ugly word treachery.'

'Your knowledge of affairs is excellent, Mr Birkenshaw, and what do ye say yoursel' in the matter?'

'Why,' said Francis, 'if you press me, I will say that I have heard that there were such virtues as honour and loyalty in the world.'

The speaker was astonished at the issue of his words. The old man's face grew white with rage, and he half raised himself in his seat. Then he fell back with a cry as the pain twinged, and lay scowling at Francis, mumbling strange oaths. 'You talk to me o' honour,' he cried, 'me, a very provost in the virtue, who for threescore years have lived wi' gentlemen o' the highest repute. And a whippit bitch o' an Edinburgh lad comes here and preaches in my lug about honour! Honour,' and he laughed shrilly, 'as if honour werena mair than the punctiliousness o' a wheen conceited bairns!'

Then as his anger passed, his face softened and he looked quizzically at Francis. 'Ye are doubtless a mirror o' all the virtues yoursel', Mr Birkenshaw, since ye talk about them sae weel. But I thought I heard word o' a daft lad in the publick o' Clachamharstan, no three days syne, whose tongue wagged to a different tune. The description I got o' him wasna unlike yoursel'.'

Francis grew hotly uncomfortable as the memory of his folly came back to him, but it roused his anger and obstinacy. He was no more to be laughed out of his purpose than terrified by a dotard's threats. So he looked squarely at his tormentor with no sign of irritation.

Then Lovat changed his tone and spoke kindly. 'Ye are a sensible man, Mr Birkenshaw, and gifted wi' some subtlety o' mind. I will do ye an honour I am little used to do to folk, and explain my exact views on this matter. It is possible that I may desire safety for my folk and honour for myself both with the highest intentions. I may have thoughts of the great old glory of my name and seek to see it bright once more in these latter days. I may have a great and patriotic policy of my own which I seek to work out through the clatter and fechtin' o' Whig and Jacobite. I may feel my own power, and ken that through me and me alone a better time can come for this auld land. I may believe all this and mair, Mr Birkenshaw; and who is to blame me if I use what tools I can summon? I have heard the word that the end justifees the means; and I can tell ye, sir, there are things better than honour, and these are knowledge o' the times and a great love for an oppressed people.'

The words were spoken in a low, soft voice and with an accent of deep pathos. The effect was nicely calculated, but once more it missed by a hair. Francis was touched in his emotions, but surprise at the recent scheme of bold impudence was still strong upon him. Earlier in the night the old lord had moved him almost to tears, but somehow this boastful romantic stuff left him unpersuaded.

'I will bring this letter to the Secretary Murray,' said he, 'whatever be the upshot. On no other conditions can I take it from your hands.'

Lovat sighed deeply, sealed the missive, and gave it to the

other. 'I maun e'en be content,' he said, 'and I trust that God will prosper the richt.'

Then his whole demeanour changed, and he lay back and laughed long and heartily. 'Sic a warld!' he cried. 'Here's a young man thinks me a traitor when he serves Murray o' Brochtoun, who could give lessons to the deil. Well-a-day, Mr Birkenshaw, get ye gone and be damned to ye for a sour pernickety Lawlander. Keep this meeting well in mind, for be sure it's the first and last time ye ever will forgather wi' a man o' intellect. But, dear, dear, Simon, ye're back at your auld boasting ways, whilk is a bad example to the young man. Tak a glass o' wine, Mr Birkenshaw, and ane o' my men will show ye where ye are to sleep. But stop, man, ye winna get through the Fraser country in sic a time without a bit word from me. This will pass you,' and he gave him one of the many rings from his fingers. 'Take it and keep it, in memory of auld Simon Fraser, who some way or ither took a fancy to ye. But I doubt, sir, ye've mista'en your trade. Ye should hae been a minister and a prop o' the Kirk.'

And with the queer cackling laughter of age still in his ears, Francis left the room.

TEN

Waste Places

The next morning before the crowd of guests were well awake, Francis had left the haughlands which lined the Firth and ridden once more into the land of storms. The image of the old lord was still vivid in his memory. Every word in their conversation, every look of that strange face, was clear in his mind, and he rehearsed the tale a dozen times in the first hour of his journey. Plainly he had been of sufficient consequence to be worth conciliating. This in itself gave him pleasure; but to temper it he had the other thought that Lovat in some way had heard of his conduct at the inn and had thought his character a fit mark for cajolery. The air of powerful cunning, of sinister wit, which the great lord seemed to bear, had left in his mind a sense of his own futility. This man had been pleased to play with him as a cat with a mouse, to talk to him fairly and treat him well; but the same man, had he so willed, could have crushed him like a child. For a little he tried to fathom his own political feeling, but could find no more than a personal sentiment. The enterprise had no charms for him; he had as little care for the Prince's success as for the Prince's person; and he saw with cruel exactness the quixotry of the whole business. But he had no mind to see any man play false to a cause with which he had linked himself; and he swore that Lovat would find himself bound to his promise. If he could reach Edinburgh before the army left for the South, it would be possible to give Murray the letter and so bind the clan to follow the Prince's standard whether the wind blew fair or foul. If he were too late, some reverse might happen which would send the Frasers and their chief to the arms of the Government. Clearly the first duty was speed.

Yet in his feelings towards Lovat much kindliness was mixed

with awe. The huge and intricate face had humour and rich nature in its crannies. He remembered the infinite changes of his speech, his heroical sentiments, his coarseness, his essays in the pathetic. The whole attitude of the man awakened a kindred sentiment in his own heart. He liked his great vigour, his rodomontade, his palpable and masterful strength. This was the man whom a month ago he would have worshipped as the perfection of the loftily unscrupulous. Now, though he was somewhat estranged from such an admiration and there was something repellent in what would once have been wholly attractive, yet enough survived to make the figure pleasing to his memory. He had a mind to help the cause which he had espoused, but if the interests did not clash, he was a partisan of Lovat's. The great lord's ring glistened on his finger, a garnet cut with a cluster of berries, and as he looked at it he felt for its giver almost the affection of a clansman.

When he crossed the river at the neck of the loch and entered the steep glens of Stratherick, he found his purpose of speed hindered. The road, which had hitherto been like a rough carriage track, was now suddenly transformed into a bridlepath among rocks and heather, sometimes obscured in bog, as often winding steeply along a hillside where a stumble might mean death. The morning had been cloudy, and now a wind from the south-east brought up great banks of wrack and obscured hill and valley. Francis had no desire to follow the devious track he had come by, for he had been told of a better path leading into the upper Spey valley and thence to the Atholl country and the headwaters of the Garry. He had planned to stay the night at the house of a cousin of Lovat's among the wilds at the source of Nairn, but the place was difficult to come at and needed clear weather. At the first sign of storm his spirits dropped, for craggy heights when cloaked in rain-clouds had still a dreary effect upon his soul. Now, as he looked, he saw the whole land grow wilder and bleaker. The glen up which the bridlepath mounted opened on a flat space of moorland, whence ran the waters of another stream on a new watershed. Down this burn lay his path, but to find it was a hard matter, when there were few marks of a track and the traveller was supposed to be guided by hilltops invisible. Just at the edge of the moss the first drizzle of rain began, and Francis looked blankly into a wall of grey vapour, rising sheer from the plashy heath and merging in the lowering sky. The air was bitter cold, and he was ill provided for a winter journey, seeing that he had ridden from the city at short notice. The man was hardy and bold, but mere hardihood is not enough to find the track in an unknown moorish country. So, bewildered and afraid, he set himself to grope his way across the desert.

Then came hours of incontinent misery. He no sooner found the road than he lost it. The rain wet him to the skin, and the wind buffeted his face till he was half dazed, and ever and again he would find his horse floundering in a hag and panting miserably. The moor was seamed with craggy watercourses, and once astray from the track he could not tell what awful ravines lurked below the white shroud. The mere constant looking-for of danger became a bodily discomfort. His eyes were strained and aching, and his head seemed to swim with his incessant vigilance.

At last the flat ground ceased and he felt dimly that he was descending a slope. He could hear a loud rushing as of a multitude of streams, but the mist hid all from view. Sometimes the noise grew louder, sometimes it seemed to die away, and only the slipping of the horse on the sodden ground saluted his ears. He was cold, wet, and hungry, and now he began to be eerily afraid. This could be no path; he must be astray in this chaos of fierce hills, where precipice and loch barred the traveller's way. By a resolute closing of his thoughts he kept his head, and gave all his care to holding up his horse. Meantime that strange din of waters was never silent: now and then he seemed almost on the edge of a great stream; but nothing appeared save the white wall and the wet earth beneath.

Then the expected mischance came, and with fatal suddenness. Gradually it became clear that his horse was slipping, and that the ground beneath was an abrupt green slope where no beast could find footing. He pulled it up by the head, but the time for restraint was over. The poor creature, with terror in its eyes and its nose between its forelegs, was sprawling down the hill ever nearer to the awful roar of cataracts. Francis after a second's wild alarm flung himself from its back and fell on the slippery descent. The horse, eased of its burden, made one desperate effort to stop, but the struggle only quickened its speed. With a neigh of terror it went over some abrupt brink into some gulf of waters. The sound of the fall was drowned in the greater noise, and Francis was scarcely aware of it till he himself, clutching wildly at the spongy soil, shot over the verge into a spray-filled chasm.

He felt a great wash of waters over his head, and then with choking heart he came to the surface in the midst of a whirling, seething pool. He made feeble strokes for the shore, but all his efforts achieved was to carry him into the main line of the current. He felt himself being whirled downward, and then with a sickening thud he was driven against a rock. His left foot caught in a cranny. Down, far down, under the stream his head sank. He had no power to move his leg till by a merciful chance it slipped, and he was able once more to come to the top and ease his bursting heart. He felt his strength ebbing, and made futile clutches at every tuft of heather and jutting stone. But his hands had no power, and they all slipped from his grasp like the cords which a man in a nightmare lays hold on to drag himself from an abyss. It had soon been all over for this world with Mr Francis Birkenshaw, if the storms of the last winter had not blown a rough pine tree right athwart the torrent. The swollen waters lipped against its side, and he found himself washed close under the rugged bole. With despairing strength he gripped it and struggled till his head and breast lay over it. Then it was but a matter of time, and slowly inch by inch he worked his way to the bank and fell exhausted in a covert of bracken.

He lay for half an hour with the water forming pools at his side and feet. Then he shivered and half roused himself to ease his breath. The thought of his horse came to him; it had long since gone to death among the misty waters. He crawled to his feet and essayed to walk, and then for the first time he felt his feebleness.

His left ankle was broken, a mere trailing encumbrance with a hot fire burning in the fractured bone. His faculty of thought began to return to him, and he weighed brokenly the difficulties of his position. Speed was his aim; ere now he should have been near the house of Lovat's cousin; and instead he was lying in a nameless ravine with his horse lost and his body maimed and shaken. He felt hazily that he was very ill, and at the helplessness of it all he leaned his head on a bank of heath and sobbed wearily.

Then he set his teeth and began to drag himself from the place. A deer-track seemed to lead upwards, and thither he crawled. At the top of the chasm he saw a hill-slope to the right and a glen in front which seemed to promise easier walking. He tried hard to think out his whereabouts, for it might be that this stream flowed back to the Ness waters and in following it he would be returning upon his tracks. But his mind refused its duty, and he could get nothing but blank confusion. He had no hope now of his fulfilling his mission and scarcely any desire. All he sought was to reach a human dwelling and have rest from his agony. His body was the seat of pain, of which his bruised ankle was the smallest part. It was so bitterly cold that even in his anguish he felt the hostility of the weather. For the grey mist was drawing closer, and the land was growing mossier and rougher. Slowly, laboriously he limped through the waste, sinking up to the knee in bog pools, or falling heavily on banks of stone. He was so scourged by rain that his clothes seemed no cover to his nakedness; he felt bleached and scourged as a whitening bone among the rocks.

Hitherto he had kept a tight curb upon his wandering wits. But as exhaustion grew upon him and the flickerings of hope died away, wild fancies arose, and he was hag-ridden by memory. He began to forget the disappointment of his errand – how Mrs Murray would call him faithless and believe him returned to his old paths, when all the while the Badenoch winds were blowing over his bones. He lost all immediate recollection, and in the stress of his physical want was back once more in the old Edinburgh days, busy picturing the gross plenty of the life. Now he was wearied, wet, and famishing, and as if to point the contrast there rose a vision of reeking suppers, of rich, greasy taverns, and blowsy serving-girls. His high sentiment of the past week was a thousand years away, and he revelled in the very unctuous vulgarity and dirt. There, at any rate, had been human warmth and comfort; and in the endless moorland his thoughts were lowered to the naked facts of life.

The mist hung more loosely, and it was possible to see some yards in front, though the sight was blinded by a solid sheet of rain. Rocks and dwarf trees raised their heads like islands, and a chance bog-pool seemed so vast that he crazily fancied he had come to the sea-coast. The path was growing easier, and a flat valley bottom seemed to be taking the place of the precipitous glen. A trail of fog looked for a moment like smoke, and he hailed it as a sign of human dwelling; but as the mirage grew commoner even the comfort of delusion failed him, and a horror of great darkness grew upon his soul. His wits were growing clearer – intolerably clear. He saw the whole wretched panorama of his misfortunes, and the blank ending which stared in his face. His mind was still in the bondage of old memories, and the revulsion sickened and drove him crazy. He stopped and leaned on a crag to give himself breath, and as in a flash the memory of Mrs Murray and all her high world passed over him with disgust unutterable.

'Curse her!' he cried, 'Am I to be damned in hell for a woman's face?' He poured forth a torrent of hideous abuse to the bleak weather. But for that proud jade with her face and hair he would have been content to seek common pleasures and vulgar luxury. She seemed to mock him out of the fog, mock him with her beauty and her arrogant eyes. Passion made him half a maniac. He leaped forward with a drawn sword, but it fell from his nerveless hand and slashed his knees. 'May she grow old and poor and withered, may she be a thing of the streets, may her pride be crushed in the gutter, may she see her friends killed before her eyes, and may she be damned immortally at the end!' And then his maledictions died away in a moan of weakness.

And now the cold seemed to have gone from the air, and his body grew hot with fever. Night was already beginning to turn the white wall of mist to black, and with the darkness came a surcease of storm. In still, dripping weather he stumbled onward down the valley. Flushes of heat passed over his face. Somewhere in his head a great wheel was revolving, and he forgot the pain of his foot in telling the number of its circles. One, two, three, he counted, six, seven, one hundred, and then he wandered into immensity. Something seemed to block his path, on which he hurled his weight despairingly. He felt himself borne back, and the soft contact of the dripping earth, and the grip of a man's hand. Then the darkness deepened into unconsciousness.

A sudden flash of light pierced his brain, and he seemed to be staring glassily through his eyes. He saw light – a fire, and the outline of a dwelling. Men seemed crowded all about him, choking him, pushing him for room, and laughing with idiot laughter. One held a point of light in his hand, which seemed the gold of a ring. Hazily he was conscious that this was his ring, which Lord Lovat had given him, and even in his utter ruin of body he felt the aching of the finger from which it had been roughly pulled. He cried for it like a child, and then the whole concourse seemed to leap upon him and stifle the life from his heart.

The days passed into weeks and months while Francis lay helpless and raving. Once he awoke and found himself on a bed of brackens in a low-roofed, smoke-filled hut. Snow blocked the window, and he saw that it was the winter time. But the thick odour of the peat reek choked him, and he sank again into that terrible deep slumber which lies on the boundary of death.

Meantime the people of the cottage went in and out on their work, nursing cheerfully the stranger who lay by the wall. They had found him in the last stage of weakness on the hill, and might have left him to die but for the chance of plunder. And when they brought him to the light they saw the chief's ring on his finger, so in all honesty, accepting this as a mandate from their lord, they had set themselves simply and ungrudgingly to nurse him to life. They were wretchedly poor, and could give him only the coarsest nourishment. The household, five in all, consisted of the father, Neil Mor na Cromag (Great Neil of the Shepherd's Crook, as the words mean), who was a herd of Lovat's on the farthest south-east hills of his territory. There were his wife and two sons, Rory, who played the pipes ravishingly, and Black John, who was his father's helper, both tall, well-grown men, who flourished on the rough fare and toilsome life. Then there was a girl just growing to womanhood, whose name Francis never heard, for all spoke of her as M'eudail or Caileag Beg, when they were well pleased, or harsher names, Oinseach – witless or shameless – when they were angry. But for the most part they were good-humoured, for the Lovat men were genial, cunning, and abundantly humorous, very little like the red Campbells or the dark Stewarts. There was a cow in a shed not five feet from his couch, and three goats fed on the hill. Thence they got milk, and at times a kid to roast. Also Neil Mor would get a sheep for himself now and then at the gatherings of the herds, when he tossed the caber a yard farther than any other, and he would sometimes take deer on the mountains and trout and salmon in the river. At times he even went down to the corn country, and bought bolls of fine meal, which all relished after the tiresome diet of flesh and herbs. But they prospered all of them on the fare, and grew ruddy, full-blooded, and straight of limb. All the day the menfolk were out on the hills, while the women cooked meals or carded wool in the firelight. Then at night Rory would get out his pipes and play springs which set the feet trembling, or sad wild strains of the men of old and the great kings of the North and the days that are gone. Sometimes, too, he played a lilt of the fairies who dwell in the greenwood and the crooks of glens, and the listeners would hush their breath and look to the barring of the door.

In the height of his illness the people of the cottage had given Francis up for dead, and walked with stealthy step and spoke softly as befitting those with death in the house. The winter was mild, but some blasts of snow came from Monadliadh, and made the women heap on peats and wood and choke the room with smoke. All this was little good for the sick man who lay wrestling with fever. They had dressed his ankle and put it in the way of healing; but the more dangerous ailment was so little known to them that they came near to killing him altogether, for they used to bathe his brow with cold well-water, and allow him to toss the coverings from his body. But for his extreme strength he would have died in the first week. As it was, the fever burned him to a shadow and then fled, and he was left with just sufficient life to struggle through. For two days the spark trembled; then his eager vitality triumphed, and slowly he began to mend.

The people had little English, and they were so far from the chief's dwelling that they heard nothing of what happened. Francis in his ravings had often mentioned Lovat's name, and they heard it with nods of recognition, arguing that this was some trusted friend of the great lord. When dawning consciousness brought him power of speech, the whole futile tale of his misfortunes was clear in his memory, and he realized how bitterly he had failed. He strove to find out the turn of events from his hosts, but one and all they were ignorant. They knew dimly of a certain Tearlach, who was said to be a Stewart and a king, and they had heard that all the Rannoch and Atholl men and the western clans had taken the field with him. But it was as nothing to them, for the old kings of Scots had no place in their mythology, which embraced so many other kings, and no straggler of Tearlach's had ever strayed to their door. But they told him of other things, all the simple talk of their narrow world; and strangely enough, these men who had rescued him with designs of plunder now cheered his recovery as if he had been their own blood-brother. Rory would play him soft, low tunes on the pipes, and John would tell of the days of herding and hunting; and everyone waited on him with grave, silent courtesy.

But on the girl fell the chief share of his entertainment. She was little compared with her tall brothers, but wonderfully slim and active, with eyes like sloes, hair blown over her brow, and a crooning voice. In the early days of his recovery, while he still lay on his back, she would give him food and bend over him with strange Gaelic caresses in the frankness of innocent pity. She was never more than half dressed, for indoors her breast and shoulders were always bare, and outside a plaid was all their covering. Then as he grew stronger and the early spring came, he would lean on her as he hobbled out of doors, and sit by her side on the green bank above the stream or in the midst of birches on the hill. As colour came back to his cheeks and some of his old vigour to his frame, it may be that the child fell in love with the tall stranger. Be this as it may, no thought on the matter ever crossed his mind. He endured her pitying caresses and the warm touch of her skin without a tremor. He had never been the prey of such emotions, and now he was something less than before. The fever had purged him of much of his old fervour, and raised, as it were, a bar between this new man and his old life.

The one thing which survived strong and vivid from the wreck of memory was the image of the lady who had sent him on this errand, and even in the thoughts of this goddess his former boyish sentiment had departed. It was a grave, old-featured man who looked down the glen of an afternoon and prayed for the return of full strength and tried to redd the tangle of his affairs.

Then at last it befell that one evening Neil Mor returned from a lambing visit to the Nairnside with news. Tearlach had come again, this time from the South, with a tail of dhuine-wassels and Sassenach lords, and a following of Macdonalds and the like. Also the folk said that the Southron forces were waiting for him in the North and that a great battle would be fought ere the moon was old. Francis puzzled over this word, and by dint of counting the weeks of his own illness, guessed at the truth. Some great misfortune had overtaken the Prince in the South, and he had returned hither to make his stand. His services might still be wanted. The whole news was so vague that he might yet have the chance to fulfil his errand. So with new hope he set about brushing his garments and preparing for the way.

ELEVEN

The Prince's Cabinet of War

Black John set him some miles on his road leading him down glen and up corrie till he brought him out on the strath of Nairn. The day was warm for a northern spring, and the guide grew exceedingly cheerful and hymned the joys of war. 'There will be braw battles,' he cried, 'for all the craws will be fleeing north, and they are the birds that ken.' Sometimes they met a lonely shepherd, and then John would stop for a parley in Gaelic and leave Francis to find the path for a mile or so alone. But when once they sighted the broad river valley, he left him with shrill farewells. 'If seed o' mine meet seed o' yours,' he said, 'brothers they sall be,' and he spat in his hand and clasped his parting guest's.

And now it was clearly the seat of war, for the tracks in the vale were rough with ruts and all the meadowland was trampled. There were few houses in the land – now and then a turf shieling on the brae-face and once the grey wall of a castle, but the place was Lowland and habitable contrasted with the wild country he had dwelt in. He had already walked far, and soon his head began to swim with faintness. It was a long toil for a man so lately sick, and it was with many pauses and long, helpless reclinings on the wayside heather that he made the journey. He had a desperate fear of falling ill a second time – a thing bitter to dream of now on the very skirts of war. And yet his hopes hung on the frail thread of his strength, so with circumspect and elderly care he nursed his body, choosing dry places to lie on, drinking but moderately from the hill burns, and sipping the whisky which he had carried out with him from the morning.

One man only he met in all that green, silent vale. This was a pedlar with a pack, a man seemingly half-witted, but to Francis' delight able to speak Scots easily. When he met him he was swinging on, with a vacant eye on the hilltops, singing some nonsensical catch. He was about to pass without noticing his presence, but Francis stopped him short and asked him the way. Clearly there could be no danger in getting news of the land from a crazy packman.

'Saw ye any soldiers,' said Francis, 'as ye came up the water?'

The man with difficulty cut short his stargazing and looked at the questioner.

'Sodgers, ay; sodgers, mony,' said he, and he went on with his singing—

> 'If ye hae plenty and winna gie,
> Besouthen, Besouthen!
> The deil will get ye when ye dee,
> And awa by southron toun!'

Francis' weariness made him cross. 'Where saw ye them?' he asked.

'There were some on the Nairn and mae at Inverness and mony mae at the Speyside,' said the man. 'There'll be war, bluidy war, and mony deid at Beltane.'

'Then where is the Prince's army?'

'Whatna Prince?' said the man dreamily.

For answer Francis took him by the collar and shook him soundly.

'Give me a plain answer, you fool. Ye may be daft, but ye are none so daft as that.'

The man looked at him quizzically. 'See here, my freend,' he said, 'if ye are an honest man like me and nae moss-trooper, but traivellin' for your ain eedification, when ye meet a man in thae camsteery times ye'll let on that ye're no quite wise. It's the safest way. As for the Prince, as ye ca' him, he's in Inverness; but Cumberland's at Nairn, and they say that Chairlie will march out to Culloden the nicht to be ready for him.'

'And Culloden,' said Francis, 'where is it?'

'Ten mile doun the haughs when ye win by the hills and come to the lang muir. And guid day to ye, freend.' The man went off, and, as if anxious to keep his hand in, fell back on his old melody. Francis heard the words quavering down the road—

> 'My shoon are made o' the red-coo's hide,
> Besouthen, Besouthen!
> My feet are cauld, I canna bide,
> And awa by southron toun!'

Those last ten miles were not far from the limits of his endurance, but with teeth set fast in his lips and his knees knoitering he accomplished them. A great wide plain running straight to the sea-line lay before him. Woods seemed to rise on the far right, and to the left the dim points of spires, while many scores of miles away over Firth and haughland rose blue ridges of mountain. Not half a mile off a bald, square house stood in the waste, and all around was rough with heather and ridges of moor.

But what chiefly caught his eye was the stir around the house, an armament of men in camp, and straggling lines still coming from the North. It was already almost sunset, and fires were being lit in the hollows of the moss, and rough tents stretched on their poles. Troops of horse seemed to move about like pawns on a board, and even at the distance he could hear distinct words of command. And yet it was not the sight of a great army entrenched, but rather of a gathering of reiving bands, already in the act of moving. The chimneys of the house smoked as if it were well inhabited, and the sight of men hurrying in and out proclaimed it the Prince's quarters.

The first sentry he met was a wild man of the Camerons, who had scarce a word of English, and showed much desire to dispute the passage. As it was, he marched by his side with drawn claymore, till he handed him to a more civil clansman with many warnings. Francis found himself led through a line of bivouacs to what seemed to be the limits of a garden. Then he trod the relics of a lawn, all trampled into ruts, with the bushes torn to ribbons and field-pieces lying blackly in the twilight. At the house door two sentries in kilts stood negligently, while a dozen ragged wretches quarrelled before the threshold. From within came a great riot as of many men speaking at once, mingled with shrill wailing from some miserable women who cowered in the shadow. Even in the mysterious half-light of the spring dusk the place and people seemed tattered, dishevelled, and ill-ordered. This was no camp of a conquering force; rather the hopeless last standing ground of desperate men. Every face was pinched like his own, and their clothing sadly worn. The hollow eyes had the look of famine, and weariness blinked in their unheeding looks.

He was led through the hall up a narrow oak staircase to a room above the chief door of the house. Here he had to give an account of his errand; before 'business with the Prince' had been sufficient password. But now he must declare himself the bearer of a letter, news of moment to the Cause. He had no thought of the nature of his reception. He had his duty to do, to give the letter; this fact alone in his weakness was clear to his brain. He was months late; events to change an era might have come to pass while he lay helpless; after all, it was but an empty errand to fulfil the letter of his mission; and then – ah, then he might wander to the ends of the earth and leave the struggle. An overwhelming desire for rest and sleep was upon him, and he faced the ordeal of the council room with scarcely a thought.

Five men sat up and down the room, one at a table busily writing, another in a great armchair by the fire, and the three others taking off their boots at the hearth. The soldier – one of Cluny's Macphersons – walked to the man in the chair with a rough salute and told him Francis' errand. Then he closed the door, and the messenger advanced heavily to the company.

He in the chair was a slim young man dressed in the somewhat tarnished splendour of stained tartans, dusty lace, and dull gold braiding. His hair was powdered badly in patches, and his whole air was of unrest and weariness. Dark hollows lay below his eyes, and his cheekbones stood out so sharply that he seemed to be smiling. Something of grace, of delicate breeding and long-descended pride, lay in his mien, but he was so huddled with lassitude that one could not judge him. He looked up drearily as Francis entered, and then with the forced grace of kingship asked him his business.

'I am the bearer of a letter from the Lord Lovat to your Highness,' said Francis, and he laid it humbly in his hand.

At the word all looked more curiously, and the man at the table jumped to his feet. He was a big, handsome man, with a large, well-formed face and little twinkling eyes. Here in this land of want he seemed the one thing prosperous, for there was something lawyer-like and diplomatic in his smooth forehead and mobile, twitching lips. He stood watching his master with eager eyes as he broke the seal.

At the first look the Prince cried out and flung the letter to the other. 'Why, man, it is dated from October. The thing is months old, and you come with it here! What has delayed you, in Heaven's name, or do you think this is a fitting time to play a fool's pranks on desperate men?'

Francis heard him only as if far away. His weariness had come over him as he stood, and a sea of angry men seemed to be rising on all sides. He staggered, and caught at the table to save himself.

'Tut, the man is ill,' cried the Prince, with ready sympathy, and he poured out a glass of wine from a bottle at his elbow and handed it to Francis. 'It's ill speaking with a fainting man.'

Meantime the Secretary had read the letter carefully through with his face puckered in smiles. 'So,' he said, 'this is Lovat's confession of faith! Little he thinks that it has just reached us, or I'll warrant the Frasers would be anywhere but in the field;' and he passed it to a tall man in tartans who had risen from the hearth.

'But I am waiting on your answer,' said the Prince. 'How comes it that you are so far behind the day?'

The tall man read the letter and threw it on the table. 'It's a thing of no value,' he said; 'ye may burn it whenever ye like. But tell me, sir' – to Francis – 'how ye came to keep the thing back?'

Francis' ears were humming again, and he looked helplessly from one to the other. 'I fell ill,' he said aimlessly – 'I fell ill somewhere in the hills and am just now recovered.'

'A likely story!' cried the tall man, but the Prince bade him hold his peace. 'The man's condition speaks for itself, my lord,' he said; 'he has the look of one walking in delirium.'

'But who in God's name are ye?' cried the Secretary. 'I have never seen ye in my life, and kenned nothing of your errand to the Lord Lovat.'

Francis put a strong grip on his wits and answered him. 'It was at the bidding of Mrs Murray of Broughton that I went that road.'

'Oh, ho!' said the man, whistling softly, 'and that was one of Meg's ploys. Well, well, she kens her own mind as well as most,' and he fell to turning up a small book of memoranda. 'Here it is,' he cried, 'written with her own hand. "Mr Francis Birkenshaw sent to a great Gentleman in the North, September 29. MM." Well, Mr Francis Birkenshaw, ye have made a bonny hash of the business.'

Now Francis heard the rest scarcely at all, but the mention of Mrs Murray pierced clearly to his dazed wits. Who was this smooth, sleek man to talk of her thus? His hands itched to get at his throat.

But the Prince saved him by breaking in. 'Let the poor fellow alone, Mr Murray; it's no time for recrimination. God knows we're all in the devil's own mess, and there's not one to mend another.'

In a moment Francis' wits were awake and he was staring hard at the Secretary. This, then, was her husband. He had pictured a strong man, wise in council and great in battle, one stern, proud, irreconcilable. And this was the real thing, this man who looked almost elderly, who had the air of a cunning lawyer rather than a great captain! He had been ready to hate or worship Murray of Broughton, to resent bitterly his unattainable power or to follow him with the hopeless loyalty that bound him to his wife. Instead he found a man he could all but despise, and his heart rejoiced. If he were unworthy of the lady's glance, still more was this thing that called her wife.

'We will put off Mr Birkenshaw's story to a happier time,' said the Secretary. 'Meantime it may rejoice him to hear that the clan of Fraser has been in the field for months. No ill, trust me, sir, has been done by your misfortune, save that our deep affection for the Lord Lovat has had some time to wait for confirmation.' And he folded the letter and placed it in his pocket.

Then the men turned to other matters and fell a-talking. Francis still stood gazing at the coals and leaning on the table, uncertain of his purpose and too weary to care. He heard much talk of the mad surprise-party which Lord George was to lead that very night, and he noted that this Atholl man was the only one of the council who had the air of brisk, soldierly resolution. He talked boldly of success, and stirred the others to some hope. The Secretary sat quiet at the table, drumming with his fingers, and the Prince had risen and was walking uneasily about the room. Months of hazard had left their mark on him, for his eye had no brightness and his step halted; he looked like one on the eve of a great crisis, so much depressed by the overwhelming chance that even the uttermost defeat would set him at peace with himself. One thing burned into Francis' memory. Charles came near the window and looked out to the wild camping scene. Then he turned drearily to the fireplace. 'My lords,' he said, 'we are a little people and a poor. It is the war of the stag against the hunters.' And, leaning his head on the wall, he burst into tears in his foreign fashion, while the grave lords around him looked on wonderingly.

Then he raised his head, and seeing the drooping Francis, was recalled to his business. Calling a sentry he bade him send for Golis Macbean. 'You will be better for a long sleep, Mr Birkenshaw,' he said, 'and on the morrow you will be fresher for the difficult job before us. I will give you in charge of one of my own body-servants, who will see to your quarters.' Then, turning to the Secretary, 'And what are your plans, Mr Murray?' he asked. 'Will you stay here or go back to Inverness? I should recommend the latter, for this will scarcely be a safe place for a sick man.'

'I will go back to Inverness,' said the Secretary dolefully. 'My legs are no fit to carry me two yards. These humours of the body affect me painfully, and though I grieve to part from your Highness' side, yet I am more in the nature of an encumbrance than an aid.'

Francis looked at him and saw that, for all his air of health, the man was indeed sick, for his face flushed and paled alternately, and when he rose his legs tottered below him. But the sight of him wakened a remembrance in his mind, and he turned to him doubtfully.

'It's a small thing that I have to ask, but I promised my Lord Lovat that the letter would be destroyed when the clan came out. I have to beg you to lay it on the fire and so set me free of my promise.'

'What a daft-like request!' said the Secretary, laughing. 'It shall be done, of course, for it is not the custom of the honest side to keep incriminating scrawls. Set your mind at ease, Mr Birkenshaw, I will see it done.'

Then he hobbled from the room with many apologies. A minute after a huge man entered and bowed at the Prince's hand. 'Take this gentleman, Golis,' said the Prince, 'and see that he has some refreshment and as comfortable quarters as may be. It will be a poor recompense for his misfortunes.'

Francis followed the big man through the house into a small outbuilding where a fire burned with beds stretched round it. Here he was given food; coarse and scanty, and with the remnants of the whisky flask he washed down his supper. His attendant clearly had little English, for he sat and watched him stolidly through the meal. Outside a small rain was beginning to fall, and beat through the broken window. The place was full of the sighing of wind, and as he lay down before the sputtering fire, Francis felt that he was indeed in a land forlorn, waiting the last extremity of a dying cause.

He slept the dreamless sleep of exhaustion till near midnight, when he was awakened by a noise of men and horses – the return of the fruitless night expedition. When he woke again it was early morning, and Golis was shaking him. He felt almost vigorous; the weakness of the night before had gone, and though his limbs ached he was no longer the feeble wanderer on the verge of faintness. Golis brought him food, and when asked of the events of the night shook his head dolefully. 'It was no good,' he said, 'for the road was as black as hell and they made ower muckle noise. Some they were wantin' to go on, but Lord George he wad not agree, and the Prince, Got bless him, is very thrawn. It will have been a bad night's work for all.' And he relapsed into taciturnity.

Half in a dream Francis heard the drums and the skirl of the pipes, and found himself looking over the level moor to where it grew red with Cumberland's troops. He saw the new addition of Frasers and Macdonalds, he watched the marching of the clan regiments to position with the far-away interest of a spectator at a show. One thing he saw clearly, that the Loyalists were utterly outnumbered, and in their ragged, starved look he saw the premonition of death. Once Charles passed him and greeted him with a smile. 'You will be still too weak for this work, Mr Birkenshaw, so you had better stay behind with me and my attendants.' Then as the forenoon wore on and the enemy grew so near that he could see the outline of their features and the details of their dress, they opened a cannonade on the Highland army, which was answered as best they could. It was the signal for the fight, and as the Prince rode down the ranks with brave words on his lips, the men answered with that cheering which only the desperate raise.

From his position in the rear he saw the whole battle at his feet. A wild blast of snow came down from the north-east sheer in the face of the Highland lines. In the teeth of the storm the long ranks of the hopeless pulled bonnet over brow, set their teeth, and went forth into the mist. It was no ordered charge, for the Macintoshes had broken away without word of command,

and the Atholl men, the Camerons, the Frasers, and the Macleans followed in a tempestuous rush. As if from far off came the noise of the meeting, and then through the hail there came a glimpse of a wild mêlée and a deadly phalanx of foes. But there at least was the shock and fury of fight. On the left wing all was different. The Macdonalds stood rigid, like pawns on a board, their ranks ploughed up by the enemy's musketry, too proud to fight in their ignoble position – men with the face of death hewing at the heath with their swords in an impotent fury. In the murky weather and the loud din of war Francis could not see the close of that bitter drama. Though the Duke of Perth implored them to follow him, declaring that thenceforth he would call himself Macdonald, though their own chieftain Keppoch besought them with tears not to shame his name, the stubborn irreconcilables stood still, waiting upon death. As the whole Highland lines were broken, and clan after clan fled to the South, the Macdonalds too gave way. Not so their chief. 'My God, the children of my race have forsaken me!' said he, and with pistol and sword he rushed to his doom among the advancing foes.

In a very little it was all over. The host seemed to recoil upon its rearguards, and in a trice Francis was swept wildly back by a rabble of dying and wounded. He was separated from the Prince and Golis, enclosed fast in a haggard troop who with wild eyes and wilder lamentations staggered over the heather. Their faces dripped with blood and sweat; many were gashed to the open bone, and every now and then one sank on the ground to be trodden under by the panic-stricken. Behind was a broad pavement of carnage, up and down which rode the English horse, slaying the hale and giving the last stroke to the dying. The air was heavy with the hot, fresh smell of blood, and as they fled Francis' old sickness came back on him and he well-nigh fainted. At last the rout grew thinner as it widened out on the extremity of the moor, and with a sob of fatigue he sank in a hollow among the rushes.

He lay for a little choking with a new excitement, listening to the thunderous tramping of hooves which seemed to assault the heavens. These moments were his salvation, for the van of cavalry passed by after the others and left the moor open to the right for escape. In a little he got to his feet and looked out. The air was still dim with snow and powder, but he saw scattered troops riding up and down, and the dull blotch on the heath where the fight had been hottest. He had no plan of flight save to regain the hills he had left, haply to find Lord Lovat and share his fortunes. But when he tried to walk he found his legs bending under him, and he was dismally conscious that at this pace he would fall an easy victim to any wandering trooper.

At that moment a horseman appeared on the right, galloping hard towards him, an English orderly on a good mount, looking spick and clean even from the dust of battle. Francis, haggard and silent, crouched in the heather; it was his one chance for life, and he was desperate. The man came nearer, riding easily, with a pleased smile on his face as of a bloodless conqueror. Suddenly a wild man rose from the earth and gripped him by the leg. A pistol cracked into the air, and a bullet splashed in a bog-pool; the next instant the elegant young gentleman was rolling in mud, and Francis was trying wearily to mount the frightened beast. Lying like a sack on its back, he suffered it to bear him whither it pleased; then slowly and painfully he clambered upright in the saddle and found rein and stirrup. The horse went back on its haunches and Francis stared round the blurred landscape, seeking direction. He found it in the sight of old Culloden house rising bare on the right, and thither he turned. At the wall of the courtyard he found a party of dragoons set round a huge man who, alone and wounded to the death, still kept a fierce front to his assailants. A dozen lay around him; his head was gashed on either side, his breast bled freely from bayonet stabs, and he could scarcely stand with a broken thigh bone. Francis recognized Golis, his friend of the morning, and with a cry to him to bear up, he urged his horse towards him. After all, death must come, thought he, and this seemed a fitting place and time. But Fortune would have none of such aimless heroism. A stray bullet grazed his horse's flank and set that already maddened beast off in a wild fury to the south. Francis could only cling feebly, careless whither he went and praying vainly for some rest from this awful toil.

Of a sudden he found himself in the thick of a party riding pell-mell from the moor to the hills. A man looked up and recognized him.

'Who are ye for?' said Francis dismally.

'For the Prince,' said the man.

'And where is he?' asked Francis.

The man pointed to a little group somewhat in front, with a man in soiled fine clothes in the middle, hurried along on a weary horse led by a barefoot Highlander.

'There goes your master,' said the man, 'and this is the end of an auld sang.'

TWELVE

After Culloden

By midday the line of fugitives was in the thick of the dark hills, with Francis sitting dumb on his horse and puzzling his poor wits with vain projects. A council had been held at the Nairnside when they crossed the Ford of Falie. Thence the remains of the troops were sent to Ruthven in Badenoch, while the Prince with some dozen of a suite set out for the west. Francis went with him, caring little where he went so long as the way took him far from the accursed field. By chance he had heard the name of Fraser and Lovat linked with their destination. The words were centres round which to gather his wandering wits. Drearily he felt that as his mission had been to Lovat, so he must see it through to the end. The Cause was lost; why, then, he must perish with the Cause, and as he had drawn the old lord into the affair, he must get to his side in the disastrous climax.

But his horse was wearied and wounded, and its rider was foolish with sickness. So at the house of Faroline he began to lag behind the party, and two miles farther had given up the vain effort. In the sleet of midday he managed still to follow their tracks, but when the weather cleared in the early afternoon he saw them many miles ahead in the extremity of the glen. The sky changed to an April blue, and with the warmth and freshness his exhaustion grew less burdensome. He stopped and bathed in a roadside tarn till the mire of the battle was washed off, and then with more spirit he crossed the nick of the pass and came out on a wide, boggy moor with the square house of Gortuleg set in the middle, and a few wretched shielings jumbled into a clachan by the highway. There was no man in sight; clearly the Prince's party had but halted for a moment and gone on. The moss-pools were shining blue, and a great crying of birds enlivened the stillness, while through the midst gleamed the links of a slow stream.

The house was in disorder, for the door stood wide to the wall and from within came the shrill cry of women. The news had already reached them, and there was mourning for a lost cause and ruined fortunes. The hall was empty and littered with a confusion of cloaks and riding-gear, with half-cooked food placed at random. A little girl stood weeping by the stairfoot, and at the sight of Francis ran screaming down a passage. The place was like a house seen in a bad dream, where all things are upside down and no human being appears. But Francis was beyond ceremony. He knew the place for a dwelling of the Frasers, and here he could not fail to have news of the chief. So he climbed the stairs heavily, only to find a worse confusion above, and some dozen ragged serving-girls who fled like rats at his approach. He opened the door of a room which was empty and stripped of all furniture. Again and again he tried, but all alike were tenantless. Then at a little room in the far corridor he found the door locked and heard the sound as of someone moving within. Angry with his aimless search, he put his shoulder to the wood and drove the hasp back. As the door flew open a little chamber was revealed with a dying fire on the hearth and an old man sitting hunched up in a chair. The figure turned a quick eye to the intruder, and Francis saw with joy that it was Lovat himself.

'Come in, sir,' said the old man. 'Come in, and God speed ye if your errand be fair.' And he turned a face of such dumb misery, such baffled wrath at war with the feebleness of age, that Francis took two steps forward and then came to a standstill. He knew that he was not recognized, and, all unknown, was the spectator of the tragedy of a career.

'Come in, man, I say,' piped the old voice. 'If ye are a freend, what news bring ye o' the last dispensation?' And he turned his ambiguous eyes upon the newcomer to give a further shade of doubt to his ambiguous words.

But something caught his notice in Francis' face and awakened recollection. He pulled himself up in his chair and glared at the other. 'Is't you?' he cried, 'you, the man that played hell wi' my fortunes and set me out on a daft venture! Come awa in, Mr Birkenshaw, for 'faith ye're a welcome guest. Ye're the man of honour to be sure, and ye've come to gloat ower the issue of your wark. Ay,' he cried shrilly, 'it was your accursed tongue and your damnable clash that has been the ruin o' an auld man and a loyal people. Ye'd best see your job to the end. There's no a man in this house, nothing but greetin' women. If ye have sic an animosity to the name o' Lovat, here's an auld life wad thank ye for a speedy quittance. I kenna if ye're still for the Prince, since you gentry have a trick of keeping your honour and your pouches on the bieldy side o' the wall; but if so be ye are, here's auld Simon Fraser who wad drink damnation to the Prince for leading him sic a road. Simon's a renegade, do ye hear? He renounces the Stuarts and a' their warks. So do to him as ye think fit. Or if ye are for King George, ye see before ye a man who sent his folk to the forefront o' the battle, one who canna look for mercy and doesna seek it.' And he held out his great hands and craned his neck as if for a blow.

The sight and words sickened Francis. The trivial inflation of the talk, the luring cajolery of the eyes, were hateful to one who had just ridden from the naked terrors of war. Remorse for his share in this man's fate slipped from him like a garment; he felt relieved, but he had also the bitterness that here had gone his last friend in the North. Had he found the Lovat of his former interview he had been ready to follow him to the death; now the last mooring had been cast from the bark of his unsteady fortunes.

He turned to go, wearily, dismally, while the old lord yelled obscene reproaches through the open door. 'Gang back to the jade that sent ye,' he cried; 'gang back to the weemen, man. Ye're ower empty and nice for the warld o' men.' Then he did a queer thing, for with infinite difficulty he struggled to the window, and there watched Francis pick his way through the moss, till he was swallowed up in the smoky clachan.

Meantime that unfortunate gentleman was in a sad temper. He had seen the degeneration of enthusiasm; he had been a witness to the palpable decay of a man's spirit. The sight of the great cumbrous body, leering, twisting in an agony of fear, made him despair of life. When he came to the village he found some makeshift for an inn in a two-roomed thatched cot, where a dirty, red-haired man sold raw whisky and pointed out straw beds to forlorn travellers. Francis had great arrears of sleep to overtake, his head rang, and his limbs ached from weakness. He ate what meal they could give him, and then asked for a place to sleep undisturbed. The landlord nodded and led him to a garret between the ceiling and the thatch, where on a bed of bracken and heather those might sleep who desired rest and a hiding-place. The temper of the man was fast sinking to a dogged carelessness. In a few hours these hills would be scoured, and King George's men would be knocking at this very door. Let them come, let them take him; after all, a tow on the Carlisle walls would be a brave ending to an inglorious and hopeless life.

The afternoon was hot after the storm and drew to a quiet evening. Without on the moor broken men passed at odd times, now sitting on worn horses, now leading their mounts, or haply merely stumbling on foot. They were the rearguard of the fugitives, for in an hour after there came a lonely party of horse, picking their way with many complaints. This in turn was the van of the pursuit, and from Culloden field to the west there would soon stretch a line of redcoats, and there would be no passage beyond the Stratherick hills.

Francis slept on till the garret-loft was dark and stars twinkled through the thatch. Then there came a rattling of the ladder which disturbed his dreams. Half dazed, he saw the landlord's red head thrust up, and the landlord's dirty fingers beckoning him down. He scrambled to his feet and followed, rubbing sleep from his eyes with weary knuckles. The red-haired man wore an air of secrecy, and he noted that the one door was closely bolted. Had the man not been clearly of the honest party, it would have savoured of betrayal. But when he entered the room he saw the reason of the thing. An old fleshy man lay groaning in a sedan-chair which had been set near the fire. 'It's the chief himsel',' said the innkeeper, urging Francis forward, and retreating nervously to the back. 'It's the great Lord Lovat.'

The door closed with a clang, and the pair were left together. Francis with drowsy brain looked hard at the unwieldy presence before him. Then Lovat checked his groanings, recognized him, and cried out in the kindliest tones—

'Ye'll excuse my ill tongue in the morning, Mr Francis. I was the deil's ain plaything wi' the gout. Ach, the unholy gripes, they play hellfire wi' a man's speerit and mainners. Forget an auld man's clavers. I have come the night at sair bodily discomfort to make it up wi' ye. And oh, sir, is this not an awful thing that has happened?'

Francis drew his breath short and sat down. Culloden was still too raw in his memory to speak of it lightly. 'I have an explanation to make to you, my lord. I was a poor carrier of your letter. I had not gone twenty miles in this vile country when I met with an accident which laid me on my back for months in a hillside cottage among your own clansmen. I have to thank your ring for the hospitality. It's not a week since I recovered, and it was only yesterday that I gave the Prince your letter. The clan had been long out, the thing was so much waste paper, the Secretary said; but though the time was by, I had to complete my errand.'

He stopped, appalled by the change on the old man's face. He scrambled from his chair, seized Francis' hand, and mumbled it like a child.

'Ye havena given the letter, my dear laddie! Blithe news, bonny news. There's life in the auld dowg yet, gentlemen.' And then, as he dimly heard the last words, his mirth ceased. He flung the hand from him, lay back like a snarling dog, and gloomed from beneath shaggy brows. 'Just yestreen, nae farther back than yestreen,' he moaned, 'and I was a safe man. A merciful God stretches the doited creature on a sick-bed, and the thing defeats the purposes of the Almighty by rinnin' to the Prince, like a leevin' corp, and giein' him my bit letter. And now there's a rope round Simon's craig as sure as if King Geordie's self had tied it. Oh that a Fraser had stuck a dirk intil ye afore ye did the evil! What for in God's name was I sae daft as to gie ye the ring? Ye micht have fund fine clean caller burial in the Stratherick heather, and nae man been the wiser or the waur. Eh, hech, the auld man and the puir people!' and he sighed with maudlin pity.

Francis saw the position at a glance. The clan had been sent out while the chief thought that the Prince already had his letter. As the unhappy Cause grew hopeless they had not been recalled, doubtless because Lovat saw himself already involved beyond escape. Now, in the final desolation, on him as one of the greatest rebel lords the punishment must fall heavy. And the bitterness of it all was that but for this scrawl of a letter he might yet be safe. He himself had not taken the field; he might represent his clan's action as flat rebellion, the disobedience of a son.

'The letter seems to stick in your throat,' said Francis. 'I had mind of your desire and asked the Secretary Murray to destroy it before me.'

'And you saw it done?' cried Lovat. 'Say ye saw the damned thing in twenty pieces and I'll gie ye a' I hae in the warld.'

'The Secretary was ill and on the road for Inverness, so I dared not press him. He swore he would destroy it with his own hands, for it was not the custom of the honest party to do otherwise.'

'But did ye no see him dae it?' screamed the old man.

'I confess I did not,' said the other.

'Then it's a' up. Murray o' Brochtoun has the letter. Had it been any ither man it would have mattered little. The Prince, Lord George, Lochiel, Keppoch, they're a' men o' honour, but Murray – my God, the thing has faun intil the richt hands. Murray! His heart is as black as bog water; he's a fine, canty man, what ye ca' a pleasant fellow, but I would sooner lippen to the traitor Judas than just this canny Murray.'

The man buried his face in his hands and rocked himself in his chair.

Francis was in despair. In his heart he could not contradict Lovat's words, for he still had mind of the Secretary's eye, and he cursed his own inertness at the moment of parting. He had been culpably remiss, for he had played into a traitor's hands; and though the victim was no stranger to treachery, it was treachery of the open braggadocio kind, and no cowardly fear of his skin. But as he looked at the figure before him repulsion began to choke his remorse. This ungainly man with white hair all dishevelled and a mottled, rubicund face, who alternated between the foulest abuse and a beggar's flattery – it was hard to rise into heroics in such a cause. For a moment Francis clapped his hands to his head and looked into sheer vacancy. His wits wandered, he seemed to be leading a crazy, phantasmal life. Without was the darkness of endless moors and hideous ragged hills, men were seeking him as a fugitive, his whole course was that of a derelict without aim or hope; and within the sordid room was this phrasing chieftain, weeping senselessly or leering with the ugliness of age. He was astray on the very backbone of creation, tethered to a madman's company. The thought roused a ghastly humour, and sitting on the table he laughed shrilly till even Lovat stopped his moaning – the laughter of wits half unhinged and a fainting body.

'See here, my lord,' he cried, 'we are two men in misfortune. I have done you an ill turn, though I never intended it. But this is your own country. It cannot be hard to find faithful servants to carry you to the wilder hills where you can bide till the blast blows by, and laugh at Murray and all his kind.'

'Dinna talk,' said Lovat solemnly. 'The finger of God is upon me. I was intemperate in my youth, I loved wine and women, and now in my declining years I am carried whither I will not. I canna put foot to the ground on a carriage road, and is it like I could gang on the stanes o' Corryarrick? Forbye, I must traivel wi' mony little elegancies and necessaries for the toilet and the stamach. I am no rude barbarian, sir, to be ready to flee at a

moment's notice. I am an auld man wi' an uncommon experience o' the warld and its ways, and some pretensions to fashion.
Is it no a peetiful thing that I must tak to the muirs like a
bog-blitter?'

He had raised his head and twisted his extraordinary face
into an expression of grave sorrow.

'I do not presume to advise your course,' said Francis. 'I only
say that whatever you may choose I am willing to share its
dangers.'

Lovat looked him up and down gravely.

'There's some sense in that thick heid o' yours, Mr Birkenshaw.
But what will ye serve? Ye will be but another mouth to feed.'

'Also another sword in extremity,' said Francis dryly. He felt
himself bound to stand by this strange man, in whose ill fortune
he had had some hand. It was his one remaining duty, and
irksome though it was he had braced his mind to it. But this
reception of his generosity damped him sorely.

The thing so set his teeth on edge that he resolved with obstinacy to see the game to the end.

'Do you accept me, my lord?' he said humbly.

But Lovat had seen fit to change his mood. He adopted a
gushing, patriarchal kindness and welcomed him with effu-
sion. 'I accept you,' he cried. 'Ye are my one true freend, my one
support, the son of my old age. May the Lord in heaven reward
ye for standing by an auld man in the day of his affliction. I can
give ye nocht in return but my blessing.' And there and then he
pronounced solemn beatitudes on the confused Francis with
the air of a desert saint.

At the door his natural manners returned. 'Keep the door
wide open, ye gander,' he yelled. 'Can a camel win through the
eye of a needle, or an auld gross man through a keyhole?'

THIRTEEN

Crabbed Age and Youth

In two hours Francis found himself at the tail of a little troop of men heading across the hills to the North. There were four stout bearers, for Lovat could move only in a litter, three strong fellows who carried food, and one special servant of the chief – these were all the house of Gortuleg could muster. The night was moonless, but the men picked their way with surprising rapidity over the breakneck land. At first they seemed to traverse an interminable ascent, up which the bearers struggled with short breath. Then at a ridge they dipped all but sheer into a woody valley, where thickets of birch and ash made a tanglewood around a brawling river. In a little they lighted on the shore of a loch at a place where a cottage was built and a boat lay beached. The thing was rough and tarry, but four strong arms sent it quickly across the moonlit water. Then began another dreary climb, this time up a rocky cleft in the hills, where fine hill gravel made the feet slip and an incessant dust troubled the eye. Once more they were on the high moors, crossing one shoulder of hill, skirting another great barrier ridge, till Francis – East-country bred – felt a whiff of salt in the air and knew the near presence of the sea. His legs ached with travel, he had been hurried since midnight up dale and over mountain at a speed which he could only marvel at. These tall men, even with the burden of a litter, could cover their hills like a good horse on a level road. For himself he was all but broken down; only the thought of the sneering Lovat kept him from yielding to exhaustion.

Just before dawn they came to the last ridge and looked down on a green strath with a firth lying pale in the midst of it. The place looked faint and far away in the haze of night, save that in the foreground an angry glow told of burning dwellings. The men stopped and looked over the edge with scowling faces and harsh Gaelic oaths. Lovat himself awoke from his broken sleep and made shift to look down on the valley. Instantly his brows grew dark, and he cried shrilly for Francis. 'Look there,' he cried, 'that is my braw house, my ain Castle Dounie, loweing like a pharos on a rock.' His tone was half-jocular, but in a moment his rage mastered him. 'God, my lads,' he cried, 'if I had just my fingers on your thrapples, I'd thraw them fine and send your gutsy sauls to the deil that begat them.' He clenched his thick hands and remained staring at the sight. But soon rage gave place to deep self-pity, and in a little he was moaning on his back for the hours he had once dwelled in it, and calling on his fathers to pity their miserable son.

With the open daylight they shifted their course to the wilder parts, and marched with frequent pauses in the deep recesses of the hills. Lovat slept, snoring loudly under the midday heat. Francis drank of every well to ease his thirst, and followed the strange procession with no sense of purpose or hope. No one there, save the chief himself, had any English, and even though they had spoken his own tongue, it is like that he would have had small disposition to talk. The man had lost all interest in his life; cold, sickness and war had so wrought upon him that he had grown a new creature from the fantastic Mr Birkenshaw of the Edinburgh taverns, even from the punctilious gentleman of the journey to the North. Again and again through the dreary day he asked himself the cause of this mournful position. Whence had flown his hopes; what had befallen that far reaching scheme of high ambition which he had once planned to follow? Yet in the severing of each strand one remained firm. Had he looked to the bottom of that dogged instinct to share Lovat's fortunes, he would have found the lingering sentiment which inspired his whole errand. His mission had been to Lovat, a lady's lips had joined their names in one command, and by Lovat's side he would see the end of the play.

As he stumbled along, when his thoughts rose from his

immediate bodily weakness, they rested with disgust on the sleeping figure in the litter. To Francis – thin, blackavised, in the main free from gross excess – this cumbrous load of elderly flesh was indescribably repellent. He could not resist a dim affection, for the old lord had that tolerant humour, that sudden warmth of kindliness, which is no unfailing sign of charity of heart. The first interview had produced on his mind an impression of an extraordinary intellect and an abundant knowledge of life. Somewhere in him pity lurked – pity for the ruin of it all, the frustration of deep-laid plans, and the misfortunes of one already feeble with age. When he did not look at the litter he was prepared to serve this fallen chieftain to the last, but a sight of the heavy face and his nice senses revolted. Times had changed with one who had revelled once in the raw vulgarities of the Pleasaunce that now he could not abide a slovenly, unheroic old man. Nor is the explanation hard; for he had met this man when still in the first heat of sentiment, he had grouped him in his mind with the choicer figures of memory, and now he resented the degradation with the fierceness of one whose sacred places are profaned.

At midday they stopped for food, and a rough feast was spread on the grass from the stores they carried. It was good, even choice, of its kind, for the indomitable gourmand had left Gortuleg with excellent provision for meat and drink. It seemed a strange thing to be drinking rich French wines on the heather under a blazing sun, when the limbs were aching, and to Francis, at least, an hour's sleep would have been more than all the vintage in the world. Lovat's eyes brightened at the display; he fell back to his old humour, and was for quizzing Francis. But the poor boy turned on him so dull an eye that he forbore, and had recourse instead to crazy affection, which was harder still to bear. Once more the poles of his chair were raised, and the troop climbed slowly the skirts of a great, mossy hill, where the feet sank at every step and savage watercourses barred the road. Then they came to a greener country – an upland valley between precipitous hill walls, level for many yards on either side the stream, and sweet with hawthorn blossom. Here stood a shieling, a heather-roofed place of some pretensions, and the shepherd came running out and talked darkly with the chair-bearers. Lovat asked him some questions in Gaelic, and his face cleared at the replies. 'The road is open yet,' he cried to Francis. 'He says that no one has come this way for a month save two packmen from Dingwall, and that he saw no sign of any man when he went round the hill this morning. We'll jink the lads yet, Mr Birkenshaw, for the Fraser is on his ain rock, as the auld proverb says.'

The shepherd accompanied them to the glen head, while the old lord plied him with questions on his work, his kin, and his profits. 'Is the lambing to be guid this year?' he asked, and the man replied in good Lowland Scots, for he was from the south of Perth, and had another tongue than the Gaelic. Then he wandered into a string of tales about the shepherd's South-country kinsmen, and though the thing was the purest fancy the intention was kindly and the result good, for the lonely man's eyes brightened and he drank in the stories with greedy ear. Francis walked on the other side of the chair, and as he watched the shepherd's placid face, the strength and ease of his great stride, and his open front to the world, he felt a sudden envy. The hills were full of the crying of sheep; it was the time of the shepherd's harvest, the birth-time of the flocks, when a man is on his feet from dawn to sunset, striving against the weather for the life of his charge. This man spent his quiet days here in this fragrant solitude, face to face with nature and death and life, an intimate of the elements, an heir of deep mountain calm. And here was he, a poor straw on the whirlpool of events, playing a desperate game with little spirit. At other times he would have consoled himself with the thought that after all he played for high stakes in a high region where success, if won, was more worthy than in a little field. But now every vestige of self-esteem had been driven forth; his eyes looked blankly upon naked facts, and he knew himself for the puppet of Fortune.

The way had grown more perilous as the stream grew smaller,

and soon they were walled between sheer sides of rock, while water brawled far down in scooped troughs of slaty stone. The road seemed to end again and again, but always there was some passage around some shoulder of hill, some byway among tanglewood which the shepherd showed them. At length they came out on the shore of a dark lake, which ran from the shadow of frowning hills to an open ridge of moor, whence the eye could discern a wide sunset country falling to the sea. By the loch shore was a cottage, empty save for a boat which lay across the floor. The men launched it and pulled to an island near the farther shore, a place some hundred yards either way and set with wind-blown firs. Here all had been made ready for a prolonged concealment. The low hut was not distinguishable from the banks of heather, and the smoke of a fire was so sheltered by trees that no one from the shore could see a sign of habitation. Once inside, the place seemed extraordinarily large and well-equipped. There were barrels of meal in one end and dried venison hams hung from the roof. A little old man greeted them, casting himself before the chief's litter and mumbling blessings. Lovat cut him short with a word, and surlily bade his bearers lift him to a chair. The sight of this final refuge, which was like cold water to the wearied Francis, vexed him with the thought of his stone halls now the shelter of others.

Throughout the evening the place was scarce habitable for his venomous tongue. There are some men – great souls – whom no trouble can crush; there are some – little souls – who are prostrate at its advent. Lovat, a mixture of both, laughed at misfortunes, but his ridicule was filled with irritation and chiefly affected his friends. He stormed at every servant in impetuous Gaelic, for his voice had lost none of its strength, and had found with old age a harsh, penetrating note which rasped on the ears. He had out the French wine from the baggage, and drank it greedily without the common civility of passing the bottle. Francis noticed nothing, for he slept in snatches since ever he had come to the hut. But Lovat needed someone to torment in such frolicsome moods, and he preferred one nearer his own quality than his clansmen. So he woke him effectually from his slumbers, and poured into his unwilling ears much low gossip about great folk, many tales of his own wrongs, and much other scandal without point or foundation. Francis listened, patiently polite. He had volunteered to share this man's exile, and whatever the provocation, he swore to do it with a good grace. The filth wearied him, for had he not once been a connoisseur in the unbecoming, but he gave exact attention with a fixed smile, till Lovat returned to an easier humour.

A week passed in the place, and Francis would have called it years. He could go abroad as he pleased, but the country was the most desolate conceivable, a plain of broken moor flanked by abrupt treeless hills. It was a type of that cold land to which the chief loyalists were already fleeing, and round which Cumberland's lines were slowly drawing. But as yet no redcoat came to the lake shore, and Francis was left, with illimitable moors abroad and a querulous old man indoors, to pass his laggard days. The weather was broken by cold and wet, and the few bright days that intervened found a soaked and blackened country and brimming rivers. Once he shot a deer, which caused a violent outburst on the old lord's part, inasmuch as the animal was out of its proper season. The fare, too, in the cottage dwindled to poverty. The finer viands were soon consumed by the chief's improvidence, and the party were reduced in three days to oatmeal, brose, tough venison steaks, and plain water from the loch. This last was the prime grievance, for by an oversight little spirits had been brought, and though the Lovat men searched the country round, none was to be had for love or money. Lovat groaned deeply over his tasteless dishes, and, observing that Francis ate with equanimity, heaped on him the most childish insults. 'Does that mind ye o' the day when your mother fed ye, Mr Francis?' he would say. 'Parritch is halesome fare, an excellent diet for the lower classes in this land, as doubtless ye ken by experience, sir.' Then, failing to irritate him by such clumsy means, he inevitably fell back on the subject of the

Secretary and the Secretary's wife, and when the poor boy with burning cheeks marched out of doors he was pursued by a chuckle of elderly malice.

Yet with it all these days had the strange effect of strengthening the tie between the ill-matched pair. The helplessness of the one in spite of his bravado appealed to the good nature of the other. The more Lovat stormed and fumed, the harder was Francis' life and consequently the easier was his conscience, for then and only then he felt the satisfaction of the man who is struggling to accomplish the wholly unpleasant. Every hint of comfort vexed his soul, for he felt bitterly that he had marred all he had laid his hand to, and that while wiser and better men were in peril of their lives, it was a disgrace that he should be in safety. So much for his humility; but the novel virtue in his nature had not rid itself of his awkward pride. It was a torture for him to be mocked at before the servants; had they understood English well, it is probable that he would have finally revolted. A dozen times a day he found himself pulling savagely across the loch with an odious, leering face dancing in his memory. The old lord knew nothing of his family history, and but the barest scraps of his life; but by shrewd inconsequence he stumbled upon the truth not once but many times, and Francis had a hard fight of it to keep from rage. Once he was betrayed into reprisals. Lovat was on his unfailing topic of women – a topic in this case not localized, but airily, generally treated by a master mind.

'What's become o' your wife a' this time, Mr Birkenshaw?' he asked.

Now this was a subject on which Francis was open to no assault, so he had a less strict guard on his tongue, since there was no anger at heart to preach carefulness.

'What's become o' yours, my lord?' he said, in unthinking, rude repartee.

In a moment he remembered the notorious scandals of the Lovat household, and repented his words. His companion became a volcano of emotions. Screaming out curses he lay back in his seat with a purple face and eyes red and starting. His men rushed to help him, but he waved them back, and bade them leave him alone with this Lowland swine. Then for an hour he made Francis' ears tingle with abuse, ending it all with a sudden flight to the pathetic. Sobbing like a child, he deplored the ingratitude of youth. 'Me that micht be your father, Francis, an auld man that surely deserves the consideration due to a loving parent. But ye're of a piece with the rest. Auld Simon is the butt of one and all, and every midden-cock craws ower the Frasers' downfa'.' Then came a near approach to apoplexy, and Francis loosed his cravat amid maudlin upbraidings.

Two days later Francis went out to the hill to shoot hares. It was the breeding season, but necessity compelled, since the table must be replenished. He stayed out till the late afternoon, and as he came down to the loch he saw to his amazement the boat leave the island with several men on board. Horses were waiting for them at the shore, and they rode off to the deeps of the moor. Twenty minutes later he arrived breathless at the edge and pulled himself over. A dozen vague notions ran in his head: was this some treachery, an attack upon their solitude, or was it a lonely conclave of the army's remnants? When the keel touched the reeds he leaped on shore and ran hard for the hut.

In a corner of the place the servants were talking eagerly in whispers. Lovat was as usual huddled by the fire, but something in his look struck Francis as strange. His forehead was puckered into large knots, and the veins on his face and neck stood out with extraordinary prominence. He spoke to himself, and his lips were twitching with what might be anger or delight. Francis laid his hand on his shoulder ere ever he looked round, and the great face turned slowly from its meditations. 'Sit down, Mr Birkenshaw,' he said, and he spoke with a precise accent very different from the freedom of his usual talk; 'sit ye down, for I have much to say to ye.

'I have had a visit from some of our North-country gentlemen,' he said, 'who are sojourning just now in these parts.'

Francis nodded in silence.

'I need give no names, but Lochiel and Clanranald were of the number, and there were others who are no less well kenned.'

He took snuff gravely, and, for the first time, tendered his box. It marked the admission of the younger man to a great intimacy.

'We talked of the late unhappy events, and we had some words of a plan. I need have no secrets from you, Mr Birkenshaw, for I can trust you. I proposed to defend these mountains with a body of men till we were granted fair terms of war. They jumped at the thought one and all, but when I looked at them I saw their unfitness. Brave, honest gentlemen, sir, but with no brains – no sae muckle as a spoonfu' – in one o' their skulls. So I told them I despaired of it, and they rounded on me and called me a turncoat.' All this he said with a certain mournful amusement, as of one above all base suspicion.

'A wheen men o' strae, sir, I tell ye,' he went on. 'Had I been a younger man I might have thought fit to move them to my purpose and guide their efforts; but I am auld, and I can but sit and look helpless on. They upbraided me, as if I were safe and they the ones in peril. My God, sir, it's hell to bide here, to see my whole castle of ambition in the stour, and to thole these moorland vapours. And I foresee worse to come. When the redcoats warm to their work and the hunt gets hotter, it'll no be a decent cot-house for Simon Fraser, but wet bogs and heathery hillsides. But I make no complaint. It is the common heritage of unfortunate loyalists. What I have to say concerns ye more closely. The Secretary Murray was one of those who came here today.'

'Murray,' cried Francis; 'then he is recovered?'

'Recovered! Oh, in a fashion. The body still looks dwining, but that was aye a common thing with Master John, when his plans went ill. He is in a lamenting, Lord-forgie-me kind o' mood, and no the brisk crouse lad ye'll probably have mind of. But there's one thing that may interest you. He spoke sagaciously to me of the folly of the whole business, and to try him I affected surprise, declared I was wholly innocent, that the Government had no grip on me, that I would welcome the sight of a redcoat, and that I was out here on the muirs for my health. He got as thrawn as Satan. "Ye're muckle mistaken, Simon," says he. "The law has terrible long fingers, and can lay its hand even on you." It was easy seen what he meant, and ye ken now the way the wind blaws.'

'But the man may not be taken. There's every chance that he may win to France, where he'll be free from any temptation to hurt you. The man's young, and as likely to escape as any.'

'So, so,' said Lovat dryly. 'That is true enough if Mr Murray o' Broughton were willing to let Providence take His ain way with him. But what think ye o' our gentleman going to meet the pursuit and giving himself up to justice?'

'And turn traitor?' said Francis, in amazement.

'Ay, just that,' said the old lord, 'and become one o' the fingers on the hand o' the law that he's aye craikin' about. For our gentleman's game will be like this. Barisdale, Clanranald, and the others gang north and west. Mr Murray gangs south under pretence of finding shelter in the Appin country. But at the first chance he is south of the Forth, in his ain house of Broughton, where the Government finds him, a melancholy man, lamenting his pitiful follies. What can they do wi' such a penitent but take him into favour, and in the course of private conversation it comes out that he has a bit scrawl that incriminates a great Highland lord whom they have long been seeking. So Mr Murray gets a free pardon, and this Highland lord, if they lay hands on him, will even get his heid chappit off' – and he laughed wildly.

Francis' face was hot with dismay. 'Forgive me, my lord,' he cried, 'if I have been the cause of your peril.'

'Nay, Francis, I dinna blame ye. Indeed it is me that has to ask your pardon, for I have been an ill companion on these traivels. But now I can at least die with a clean hand and a proud heart. It shall never be said that a Fraser, though feeble and stricken in years, was feared o' the whole black gang o' them. "*In utrumque paratus*,"' he quoted with inimitable gusto, '"*seu versare dolis, seu certae occumbere morti*."'

Francis went to bed, but not to sleep. The image of the savage, heroic old man, his hypocrisy discarded, fronting death with equanimity, was burned on his mind. A fierce anger against Murray possessed him, and as he thought of what one proud woman would think of such conduct, and all the misery which awaited her, he groaned in bitterness of spirit. But his wits were clearer, now he had a plain duty before him, something which an active man might effect without presumption. Above all, now was his task more closely connected with her who had been his task-mistress. Henceforth he wrought for her direct, palpable good.

In the grey misty morning Lovat was wakened by the young man standing at his bedside.

'I have come to make my farewells, my lord, for it is time for me to be off.'

'Are you like the rest then, Francis, and leave the sinking ship?'

'You know well enough to the contrary, my lord. I go to seek the Secretary.'

'Good lad,' said Lovat, 'but how will you find him? I ken nothing of his road save that he went south by Appin.'

'Then I will go to Appin, and maybe I will get word of him there.'

'And then, when ye get him . . . ?'

'Why, then,' said Francis, 'Mr Murray and I will have words, and a certain bit of paper will find its way to my pocket, or I will ken the reason why.'

'It's a great plan, Francis,' cried the old man, 'and God speed your hand. Shake the tod weel, once for me and once for yoursel' and once for his leddy wife. If I never see ye again in this world, I'll see ye in . . .'

But the place was empty, and Francis was gone.

FOURTEEN

How Mr Francis Came to the
Lowlands Once More

At this point the industrious narrator passes from a sober tale into the realms of wild romance. Nor can he help himself. For take a wild young lad, or rather a serious man still in his youth, whose mind has been strung high by vain enthusiasms, who is spurred by a desperate hope. Conceive such a one to have climbed with difficulty the first steps of the ladder of virtue, to have curbed his fervours, to have bowed before the eternal commonplaces of love and duty, to have found himself in a difficult and unmanly place, and now at last to have a chance of honest deeds. Suppose him strong in body – for the weeks in Lovat's hut had restored him – give him a plain task, a sword at his side, not a word of Gaelic, the mistiest notion of the hill country, and burning cause for speed – and you will find that he will run into many stone walls ere he pass the Highland line.

With Lovat's directions he came to the Linnhe coast and met no mishap. The way had been a terrible toil over a birk-clad moorland and bare scarps of slaty hill. Finding some poor fishermen on the beach, he slept the night in their hut, giving them a piece of Lovat's money in payment for the oatcake and dried fish which they put before him. The men were honest and considered the payment ample, for they took him aboard the lugger and set down the loch to one of the long water-arms which run into the east. He repeated the name Appin, at which they nodded to the beach; and when he found himself ashore he comprehended their gestures, recalled the old lord's directions, and realized that this was indeed Appin. That night he slept on the moor in a ditch among heather, and at daybreak was on his

way in a pleasing land of green valleys, where the smell of salt
hung over bent and tussock. By the afternoon he had come to
the house which he had been bidden to seek, the house of John
Roy Stewart, called sometimes John Howglass and sometimes
John of the Hairy Legs. The man was kin to the Fraser, and –
what was far above pedigree – had some little English. When
Francis had eaten his fill and slept heavily for some hours, he
put the question to his host.

'Murray?' cried the man. 'Murray never came here, though
he sent a man to beg from me while he was hiding by the Leven
Loch. That was a week syne. Murray darena show his face in
Appin, for ten years back he had a kind o' bicker wi' Ardshiel,
and it's kenned that the Camerons canna thole him. Faith, it
would be a back-cast of the Lord's hand that sent Murray to
Appin, and Sim maun be failing in mind or he would have had
the sense to ken that.'

'It was Murray's own word,' said Francis.

'And Sim believed him! Dinna tell me that! Na, na, your
gentleman will be skelping lang ere this ower Balwhidder braes,
and he'll soon be casting his coat in his ain house of Brochtoun.
That's to say, if ye read him richt, but I confess I had a juster
notion of the man.'

'If he's gone south, then south I must go,' said Francis.

His host propounded to him a choice of roads. He might go
south by the Campbells' country, take a chance of a ferry over
the lochs, and come to the right shore of the Clyde above
Dumbarton. Thence lay a level ride to Broughton in a quiet land
among Whiggish countrymen. Or he might go straight through
the wilds of Awe to the young streams of Forth and enter the
Lowlands by Lennox or Lanark. Francis chose the first, and so
all the next day he strode through the green country of Appin in
a land channelled with bright streams and filled with the noise
and scents of the sea. Few of the people had been out; but it
was a miracle that he passed unchallenged, for the place was
watched jealously by its neighbours of Lorn, seeing that of old
Campbell had been at war with Stewart. At night he came to a

herd's dwelling on a lonely hill, where his path turned inland. The man gladly kept him the night on the mention of John Howglass, but again it was a monotonous feast of silence, where he sat and smiled into the eyes of a friendly tangled giant.

The weather still kept calm and blue as he struck the next morning into the remoter deserts. Twenty miles straight by the south-east wind, John Roy had said, and he would come to the sea. But Francis had little hillcraft, and it may be that the twenty became thirty ere he looked down on a dark sea loch, sleeping between strait mountain walls. All day he had met not a soul, save that an hour before midday he had seen two figures on the skyline of a hill at the head of the glen in which he patiently stumbled. They, too, seemed to have caught sight of him, for instantly the place became void. This was the one warning he got that he was in a country of war; but he was puffed up by the ease with which he had won thus far, and forgot the thing the minute after.

Ere he came to the shore he learned the moral of the figures on the hilltop. As he slipped heavily from rock to rock down one of the shallow corries which dropped on the sea, a bullet suddenly sang by his ear and bored into a bank of sand. He had the sense to lie prone in the stream and pray that the shot might have been intended for other game than himself. But the noise of feet on the stones spoiled his hopes; he was too footsore to run; so he surrendered helplessly to three ragged men who leaped on him from above. One who had some words of English asked, 'What ta devils he was crossing ta Cruart Vhan so hotfoot?' but Francis' reply sounded deeps of language unknown to him, and all that was left was to hurry the unhappy captive along the hill-face, till his arms seemed torn from their sockets with rough handling.

How long and how far he went he soon lost power to guess. His shoes were filled with small sharp stones which galled him severely. He struggled to prevail on his guides to slacken pace, but their only reply was deep, convulsive laughter. At last their path was barred by a glen down which a salmon stream roared to the Firth. At its foot was a rude fisherman's hut – a few stakes and boulders with a roof of turf – which seemed to be the goal of the violent journey. At the door stood a personage dressed in plain Lowland garb, save for a magnificent scarlet hat which surmounted a very well-kept periwig. The three men greeted him with the most abject reverence, and pushing Francis forward left him to explain the posture of affairs.

'And who may you be, sir?' said the great man, tapping a snuff-box and looking with disfavour at the three dirty Highlanders.

'I have yet to know by whose orders I am held prisoner,' said Francis, 'and who it is that has the right to ask me.'

'Hoity, toity,' said the man, 'heard ye ever the like? Are ye aware, sir, that this is the Campbell country, and that I am the Duke's own cousin? Do ye ken, sir, that the Campbells, serving as they do the lawful king, have a warrant to search these hills for any members of the disaffected clans or Lowland rebels who may be lurking there? And ye question my right!'

'I ask your pardon, my lord,' said Francis with diplomacy. 'I am glad indeed to find allies in a good work. I am at present in pursuit of a notorious Jacobite, one John Murray of Broughton, who is known to have come from Appin southward through this very country; and if you can enable me to lay hands on him I will be everlastingly your lordship's debtor.'

The man was vastly flattered by the tone – still more by the title.

'Then it is my part to ask your pardon for the unseemly conduct of my poor people, Mr . . .'

'Birkenshaw,' said Francis, speaking the truth at random.

'And if it turns out to be as you say, and I doubt not it will, I will aid you with all my heart. Meantime I must beg your company to sup on such poor fare as is here provided. My uncle of Inverforth will be here in three hours' time, and he will explain matters to you more fully.'

'Three hours' grace,' thought Francis, for before Inverforth he must stand unmasked, seeing that he had no tale to meet the ear of one who had been at Culloden and was famed as the bitterest foe of the Prince's in the land. Before three hours' time he must give this gaudy gentleman the slip, and with the help of Providence put the loch between himself and his pursuers. He had noticed a boat on the beach; if he could but reach it, he was safe. Once over the water and he was not far from the confines of settled country, if he minded John Roy's words aright.

They supped daintily on fresh-caught salmon, hill mutton, and some bottles of foreign wine which the man fetched from a store in the hut. The Campbell talked volubly on a score of subjects, as if glad to find one less barbarous than the hillmen to listen to his elegant talk. Francis humoured him as far as he was able, and bandied the names of great folk to his own admiration. Three several scandals linked with the name of Lord Craigforth did he invent on the spur of the moment, and tell to the greedy ears of his companion. He had to listen in turn to many weary recitals of slights and successes, of days in Edinburgh and London where it seemed that Mr Campbell had played a great part, and a minute account of the interminable Campbell pedigree. Meantime he feigned exceeding interest and a growing fuddledom. His cheeks flushed and he rubbed his eyes, blinking. Then he complained of the heat, and the effect of wine on one who had been so long without it, paying a compliment to the strong head of the other. He wound up with a request for a second's walk in the open. 'I am somewhat confused with my long journey and the strength of the Bordeaux. Three turns on the heather will set me right, so I beg of you to excuse me.'

Mr Campbell, himself approaching hilarity, was graciously pleased, and in a second Francis was on the moor and out of sight of the gillies. The loch lay purple-black, for the night was moonless, but a line of pale light marked where the stream entered and the boat lay moored. A minute, and he was there, feeling for the chain and the stone to which it was fastened. To his chagrin the thing was padlocked, and passed through a stout ring of iron in the boat's stern. He searched for a weak spot but found none, nor could he move the great stone which did duty for an anchor. Despair seized him, and he tore at the thing like a madman. The ring creaked, then as the tugging grew fiercer the stern planks shivered, till at last the wood gave and he found himself sprawling with the chain in his hand and a ragged end of timber encircling the ring. The noise was loud enough to be heard across the loch, so in a fright he scrambled into the boat and put out the oars.

He could hear men come crying from the hut as he shot into the blackness. If this were the only boat, he was safe enough; but he dare not risk the nearest point of the far shore, but drew down the water as he guessed its direction. The mountains rose wall-like in inscrutable night, towering into the blacker arch of the high heavens. He scarce could see the tips of his oars, scarcely the murky water beneath; he felt like one entering into a fantastic land without law or limit and yet he was no more weary, but extraordinarily light and active. Then he heard in his wake the plash of oars; the gillies must have found another boat and be giving chase. He was hailed in strident Gaelic by some angry man, and then the world was quiet save for the monotonous sound of rowing. Francis grew perfectly cheerful. Often on the Fife coast had he played at this game – on an angry firth and not on a placid, landlocked sea. He could tell that the boat behind was not gaining, for though there seemed to be two men at the oars, it must he heavier and coble-shaped, whereas his was an elegant pleasure-boat

But as the minutes passed and the chase continued he began to cast about for a refuge. If he turned into the shore, they would follow; and now, as his arms grew sore, he could not hope to put such a distance between them and himself as would suffer him to land unnoticed. His wits failed him, and he could think of nothing. Wild schemes of upsetting the boat and swimming ashore flitted across his mind, but a remembrance of the width of the loch as seen by daylight warned him to prudence. Even in darkness his pursuers could track him easily by the sound, so he could not hope to baffle them by any ruse of turning. Suddenly a chance arose for his salvation. The outline of a ship all blurred with night leaped up on his left, apparently not more than twenty yards away. Here was a case for neck or nothing. With a moment's thought he kicked off his shoes, tossed the oars into the water, and dived overboard, and a minute later was clambering up the bowsprit of the vessel.

He ran down from the bows to the deckhouse, picking his way amid a multitude of ropes and bales. The door was shut, but a light came through the foot, so without parleying he opened. A man sat alone at a table, working out some figures and sweating with the toil.

'Francis Birkenshaw!' he cried in amazement, as he saw his visitor.

Francis stared; then 'Andra Gordiestoun,' he stammered, in open-mouthed surprise.

'So ye've taken to this trade,' said the captain sourly. 'I suppose ye will be for him they ca' the Chevalier.'

'Indeed I am,' said Francis.

'I micht have jaloused it. Ye were a blagyird in the auld toun o' Dysart, and it's no like ye'd be convertit on the Hieland hills.'

'There's a boatful o' men behind me,' said Francis. 'Are you minded to give me up?'

'To be sure I am,' said the man; 'I am a decent supporter o' the King – God bless him – and I'll hae nae rinaway Jaicobites on my vessel.'

At the moment there came a great crying from the bows, as the pursuers came up with the deserted boat and the moored ship. The men hailed the captain in their scanty English, and Francis sat down despairingly to await the issue. The conversation – heard in snatches – was of a kind to cheer and surprise him. For the captain argued, first, that no man had come aboard; secondly, that if one had, it was no business of theirs; and, thirdly, that they might be damned for a set of dirty Highland beggars, and, if they stayed longer, he would rouse his men and send them and their boat to a better place. Which last point – and the gestures and tone which accompanied its deliverance – was found so convincing that the party retired in haste.

'You're better than your word, Andra,' said Francis, on his return.

'Say nae mair about it,' said he. 'And look ye here, Mr Birkenshaw, ye may be a michty scoondrel, as I have nae doot ye are; ye may be fresh frae cuttin' the throat o' Maccallum Mhor himsel'; but ye come frae my ain toun, and I have drunk mony glesses wi' ye at the harbourwalk, so I'll see ye through wi' this bit business, if it does na interfere wi' mine.'

'If you can put me in by the Renfrew shore you will do me a great obligement.'

'And it so happens that that is my very road,' said the captain, 'so the Lord has lookit after ye better than ye could guide yoursel'.'

As Francis lay down in a ship's berth he could hear the anchor lifting, and soon they were dropping down the loch with a light breeze behind. When he awoke late in the morning, they had already left it and were making their course by the south end of an island in what seemed a broad sea, lined on one side with craggy hills and on the other by far-stretching lines of level country. For the whole of a long day they made slow progress up the Firth, tacking against a difficult wind, while Francis looked idly from the bows, busy with his own reflections. The skipper was always by his side, leaving him only to make short inroads below or to yell orders to his men. To his amazement Francis found that he was no more the godless Andra Gordiestoun of the old days, but an enthusiast in religion on the watch for a proselyte. True, his language was violent as ever, and he seemed little less drunken; but his talk was always of theological myster-ies, and texts fell easily from his lips. He preached Francis a vehement sermon on the error of his ways, adjured him to flee from a wrath to come, painted that wrath in awful colours, and dwelt zealously on the joys of the redeemed. Francis heard him out with impatient grace. He himself had been the arena of so severe a struggle, good and evil had fought such a duel in his breast, that he was willing to lend an ear to anyone who could teach him the way of life. But these phrases, this fluent rhetoric, seemed paltry to one whose soul was scarred with a grim reality, he was in the actual throes of a vain endeavour; little to him these commonplaces of the throng. And yet this man, sent with such words out of his own tattered past, was a sting and a remembrance of years misspent.

'I will pray for ye, Francis,' said the man, on parting, 'that ye may yet be reclaimed. It's a puir warld withoot hopes o' a better.'

'I say "Amen" to that,' said Francis, as he stepped ashore on Lowland earth.

BOOK III

FIFTEEN

The House of Broughton

By the afternoon of the next day Francis had put many broad Lanark and Renfrew cornfields between himself and the sea, and had come to the upmost streams of Clyde, where the land begins to fall away towards pleasant Tweeddale. He had bought a horse with some of his Highland gold, since his business demanded speed, and ridden through the quiet Whig clachans with none to gainsay him. Only at the change-house of Roberton did he stop to wet his dry lips with ale. The landlord was an honest, sunburnt countryman, so Francis ventured a question.

'What like is Tweeddale now that the steer is over? Are there still Murrays to vex it?'

The man looked suspicion for a second and quietly stroked his right cheek. By luck Francis knew the current Jacobite sign and responded.

'I ken but ae thing o' the estate o' affairs in Brochtoun,' said the man. 'The Leddy was bidin' there hersel', but yestreen yin came bye on a blae horse and syne yin on a broun, and I think the last was awfu' like the shape o' the Laird. Hae ye ony word yoursel'?'

'None save that soon there's like to be a flittin' from Brochtoun House.'

'Across the water belike?' said the man.

'Maybe scarcely so far,' said Francis.

'But he'll ne'er be ta'en. Brochtoun's a dour bit, but the lave o' Tweeddale is leal and no Whiggish ava'.'

'I have naught to tell you,' said Francis, 'but if you do not hear within a week that Mr John Murray went up the Edinboro' road wi' a company o' dragoons to keep him cheery, then thank God for saving a poor gentleman from himself.'

The flush of early summer was on hill and wild-wood as he rode from the green moor road into the shadowy vale. To one sick of rock and heather and the sour, unkindly odours of moss and torrent, the place seemed goodly beyond dreams. It was mid-afternoon, and in the mellow glow all was softened, touched with enchantment and old romance. The glen was asleep; scarcely a murmur of water reached his ears; the white stone cottages by the meadow-edge, the grey walls of the Place among the trees, the faint lines of far-away mountains – all were part of an ancient primordial peace o' the world. And the air of the place bewitched him till he lost all settled thoughts. Before, he had been puzzling sore over the knots in his destiny and striving to form a clear plan of conduct. Now, he was in a fairy-land of sentiment, where a woman's face shone ever from the still and golden skies.

He came on the Edinburgh highway above the bridge of the burn, some hundreds of yards from the road to the Place. His heart began to beat painfully at the thought of the near meeting. The whirligig of time had been playing pranks since that morning a year before when he had ridden down Edinburgh streets to the North. And what had been the end of his mission? Dust and ashes! He had no news but the worst, news of treachery, of suffering and black fortune. Was she likely to find pleasure in his presence for all his highflown dreams of service? And at the thought Francis brought his horse to a walk and braced himself for the inevitable.

Suddenly, at a turn of the bridge, he came full before the eyes of a party of three who were riding leisurely towards the great avenue. They turned round at the sound of steps, and his heart stood still, while he felt the blood palpitate about his forehead. For the meeting he longed for and dreaded had come. The lady rode between two tall, harsh-faced gentlemen, one a grey-headed man with a soldier's bearing, the other younger, but with the same grim, narrow features. A far-away resemblance in the eyes made him hastily set them down as kinsmen.

At the sight of him the lady's eyes grew wide with wonder,

and she involuntarily drew rein. Then she nodded to her companion.

'Wait for me, Henry,' she said, 'I have a moment's business with this gentleman,' and she turned and cantered to the bridge end.

'You have returned, Mr Birkenshaw,' said she. 'Have you any news for me?'

For a little Francis could only look. Her face was so pale and thin, her eyes so impenetrably sad, that he was lost in pity. Then, 'I took your message to the Lord Lovat,' he said lamely, 'but was prevented from returning by a sore sickness. I saw the Prince on the eve of Culloden, and was by his side in the battle. I followed him to Gortuleg, and there, finding the Lord Lovat, I conceived it to be my duty to attach myself to his cause. Now I am come from him on a matter which closely concerns yourself.'

'You have done well,' she said. 'I heard that you had reached Lovat from other sources, and when no further news came of you, I had thought you were dead. I am glad to see you safe. But I cannot wait longer lest I make my friends impatient. You have done my errand loyally, and I thank you from my heart. I would offer you the hospitality of my house were it not old and half-dismantled; but the village inn will receive you for the night. I will lay no more toilsome missions on you. Farewell, Mr Birkenshaw.' And ere he could say a word she had ridden up to the others.

Francis' heart sank to the ground. This was the dismissal, the end of his long service. For this he had endured sickness and weariness, cold mosses and the cruel hills. She had used him only as a servant, when he had thought he was a friend. His humiliation was bitter, his disappointment so utter as to benumb his mind. In a state of dreary bemazement he turned his horse's head to the village.

But he had told her of private news, and she had not waited to listen. What woman, least of all what woman of her eager temper, could have acted thus? And then her talk of the inn

– and with this, light broke in upon his brain. She had feared suspicion on the part of the two sour cavaliers. She had to all intents bidden him go to the inn and await her further commands. Clearly she would find ways and means to visit him. The thought was so comforting that he fell into a state of unreasoning joy. She seemed solitary and friendless; then he, and he alone, would right her wrongs. This pale-cheeked lady was not the glorious beauty he had left, but she was something finer, subtler, more enchanting, pure gold refined in the furnace of sorrow.

The landlord of the inn was changed, the stout old Whig being dead, and a zealous Murray's man reigning in his stead. He eyed Francis with undisguised annoyance, clearly suspecting the designs of a stranger so near a noted harbour of the outlawed. Nor did Francis improve matters by his cunning questions to find out the man's leanings. The host adopted a robustious Whig tone, and professed a violent love for Hanover and all its appurtenances. This compelled the other to a like avowal of loyalty, and soon the two stood in a posture of mutual suspicion. Then the main purpose of his errand began to stir in Francis' heart, and he asked cautiously about the Laird's whereabouts, if haply he were yet lurking in the place. The man affected secrecy and drew him aside.

'Ye ken the top house in the clachan,' he said. 'Weel, that's John Bertram's, and at its backside is a bit gairden. There abune the tattie beds is a kind o' hole in the solid rock, whaur Murray has been hiding thae twae days.'

The news fired Francis to action. Could he but get speech of Murray all might yet be well, false faith might be prevented, and the honour of a great family saved. He learned his directions from the man, and made his way up the fields to the garden back. With some pains he pierced the thick thorn hedge and found himself in a lone strip of ground, half planted with greens and half the bare rock of the hill. By dint of much searching he found a hole of some dimensions, and bearing marks of recent use. But now it was empty, utterly. When he came out he saw through the dusk a face at an open window in the cottage watching him closely. He ran down to the garden foot, but ere he reached it the window was shut and closely barred; and though he knocked hard at the back door he could get no admittance.

In some irritation he made his way back to the inn, where he found the landlord waiting with a clouded face.

'Why the devil did you send me on such a goose chase, sir?' Francis asked fiercely. 'Where is Murray?'

'Let that be,' said the man sullenly. 'Look ye here, sir. This is a letter sent you this moment from a certain lady. Now, before ye get a sicht o' 't, ye will tell me plainly your way of thinking, for I will see ye damned afore I will have this lady come to ony hurt.'

The man stood so fully revealed by his words that Francis felt the need of caution no longer. 'Why, man,' he cried, 'I am honest to the backbone. I have just come from the North with news for my lady. I was by the Prince's side at Culloden, and am not a week from my Lord Lovat's company.'

The landlord looked relieved, and gave him the note without further scruple. It proved to be a mere line to arrange an hour of meeting. Nine of the evening was the time she fixed, when with her servant she would seek Mr Birkenshaw's presence. Francis read it and dropped it into the fire.

'Perhaps you will tell me now where the Laird lies,' said he.

'Till this morning he was in that hole I telled ye o', and I kenna why he left it. He micht hae lain there canty for months. This countryside was ill inclined to him, but there's no a man wad cheep a word o' where he was hidin'. But this morning he gaed off to Powmood to his guid-brither's, and I sair misdoot if he'll find it as quiet a biggin'. The mail gaed bye the day wi' twae-three lads that hadna the look o' Moffat dealers. I wish I kent if they passed Powmood.'

Francis groaned in spirit. This was the confirmation of his worst fears. Even now the man might be in the Government's hands with all his weight of secret knowledge. His first thought was to fly to Polmood and strive by main force to arrest calamity. But it was near the hour appointed for the meeting with Mrs

Murray. Even as he waited the clock struck the half-hour; so he went upstairs to spend the thirty minutes in snatching supper.

He had finished his meal and sat watching the firelight strive with the last fading glow of day on the wainscotted walls. He felt very melancholy, what with the ruin of a great cause and the futility of his little plans. Of what worth was he after all save to follow a greater's lead? He had not it in him to originate or to command. Something of his boyish sickness for cutting a fine figure in life came back to him at the moment, and added a pang to his regrets. And bitterer than all was the thought of his mistress' sorrows, of the long loneliness and shame which lay like a pall athwart her future.

Then when he had lost all cognizance of the present and was deep in dismal fancies, the door opened and two women entered. One was a maid, a little rosy-faced countrywoman, and the other was the lady of his dreams. She advanced to greet him with both hands held out after her impulsive fashion, and before he knew he had taken them and led her to a seat. She wore a heavy dark cloak, and when at length she laid it aside, there were no bright robes beneath, only a sombre gown which made her white face paler. Her manner, too, had changed utterly. Of old she had looked at him with the sovereign air of a mistress; now there was hesitation, diffidence, the tremulousness of grief.

'You understood me, Mr Birkenshaw. I was vexed to turn from you so hastily, but my cousins of Romanno are ever suspicious. And now I can thank you for doing my work so well. In this lamentable confusion, when the best blood has been spilled like water, it is a pleasure to see a kenned face. And you will have heard, sir, I am desolate now, and have no one to look to save such honest gentlemen as serve me out of goodwill,' and she smiled a little ghost of a smile.

Francis' blood was painfully stirred. He could not bear to see her sitting there so changed from her high estate. A great tumult of compassion arose in his soul.

'And now for your news,' she said, 'for I believe you have

something to tell me in private. My maid is a sharer of all my secrets.'

Here was a quandary for the unhappy man. How could he tell this pale heroic woman of her husband's perfidy? It seemed cruel beyond thought, and his heart failed him.

'It had to do with your husband,' he stammered; 'but if –'

He got no farther, for at the word 'husband' he saw she knew all. She covered her face with her hands and her bosom heaved with her sobbing. 'Oh, it is true,' she cried. 'I am near crazy. I have fought – Oh my God! – I have fought to prevent it, but I could not. I knew his heart, but he denied it when I asked him, and put me off with smooth phrases till it was too late. And now he has gone to Polmood, and I am left to curse my woman's weakness. And he was the King's friend, the first man in Scotland to stand by the Prince, and the wisest head in his councils.' She rocked herself to and fro in an impotence of agony.

Suddenly she rose to her feet and flung herself beside him with her hands on his arm. 'Oh, save me from myself,' she cried. 'I shall go mad, I have been alone for so long and my mind is sick with care. Oh, help me, help; do not go away. The Saints sent you here today, and I have been alone so long, and I have no friends but you.' And she ended in stormy tears.

Francis was at his wit's end with perplexity. To see his proud mistress humbled pierced him to the heart. He raised her and with the help of the maid reduced her to something like calm. But all the while there was an undercurrent of crazy delight. Now at last she had summoned him to her aid, he need fear no rival in her service any more; and at the thought he felt the ragged ends of his life gather to a centre. Here lay his duty and task; his toil was but beginning.

At that moment through the window came the noise of a carriage driving rapidly along the highway to the North. It had the sound of a great equipage, and Francis instinctively drew back to the shadow of the curtain. Then came the sound of a stopping at the inn door. The three in the room looked at each other in fear; even Mrs Murray's eyes lost their vacancy.

Francis peeped through the curtain's edge, but all he could see was a splash of light in the mid-road from the carriage lamps and the open inn door. There was the sound of a man alighting, then of some talk with the landlord, in which the remaining inmates seemed to join. Then the man re-entered, the door was closed, and the echo of wheels died in the village street.

Francis rushed from the room with a foreboding of tragedy. He met the landlord at the stairhead with a face somewhat whiter than his own. There was no need of question; the man's look was eloquent of all.

'It's twae captains frae the Castle,' he faltered, 'and Murray o' Brochtoun is sitting atween them.'

SIXTEEN

A Council of Honour

When Francis came to the house on the next forenoon he found it silent as a mausoleum. The smokeless chimney, the wide avenue beginning to show traces of lack of gardening, the great mass of untrimmed blossom on wall and border, and the sealed, dusty windows seemed to tell of a masterless home. Curlews screamed over the flower-garden, and in one spot where the heather had encroached on a clipped lawn two melancholy peacocks strutted in the confusion.

The solemn maid opened the door to him and took him to the self-same room where he had sat that night a year before and waited on the lady with the lamp. The same air of lost splendour which had afflicted him without, oppressed him within – the deep rich wainscotting, the carved shelves of books, the emblazoned mantelpiece, all with a subtle atmosphere of neglect and disuse. The carpet still bore the mark of a man's mud-stained boot: here doubtless the Secretary Murray had bidden farewell to his house and his honour.

Then Mrs Murray came to greet him, and led him to a summer-room looking out upon the hill and the western valley. She was no more the distracted woman of yesterday, but composed and pale, with heroism at her lips and eyes weary of life. Francis trembled at the sight of her, for this face argued some quixotic resolve and he anticipated troublous days. Night had worked changes in his temper. He had lost his first tumultuous anger and grief; the fervours of his spirit had abated and left his soul cold and exceeding bleak. He wavered nothing from his purpose, but he would have welcomed gladly yesterday's high sentiment. What though it were but vain elation, it had at least made the world roseate for an hour. Now he was a wiser, stronger man, but one with teeth set and his back to the wall, fighting against inclination, prudence, and his own unregenerate heart.

But this new mood of his lady's matched his own, and relieved him of one difficulty. For with all his compassion he had a horror of tears, a shrinking from the pathetic; and the spectacle of a weak woman looking to him alone for aid could in certain moods arouse only repugnance. But now all dealings between the two were passionless and kindly. This tall lady was again the mistress, and he waited to do her bidding. He asked her purposes.

'There can be but one way,' said she. 'He will go to London, and there I must follow him. I cannot hope to mend matters, for I am poor and have little purchase, but I may see him and try. I have no hope, Mr Birkenshaw, but it is better to press on in some sort of endeavour than eat out my heart here in despair.'

'But where can you hide in London?' asked Francis. It was his duty to look after the plain facts in the wrapping of the romantic.

'I do not know,' she said, 'unless with my cousin, Lady Manorwater, who is of my religion, and if all else fails will take me with her overseas.'

'But how will you make the journey?' he asked.

'Why, how would I make it but alone, with my own horses and the one servant who is left me?' she said, with a faint attempt at vivacity.

'But who is to see to your lodging on the road and guide you safe through an unsettled country?' he asked again.

'Ah, I cannot tell. I must use my mother wit and there is all the need in the world for hurry,' and she twisted her hands with a sad gesture of impotence.

'And above all, my lady, is it likely that you will convince your husband in a hurried sight of him, if you failed before his arrest when you had leisure and safety?'

'I can but try,' she said simply. Then, 'Oh, Mr Birkenshaw, the thing is less a journey of hope than of despair. I will know that I have left nothing undone, and that may be a solace in the dark years that remain to me.'

She spoke so sadly that Francis was moved, and the old sentiment began to rise in his heart.

'I owe a duty to – a great Highland lord,' he said, 'which I must sometime fulfil. If you go to the South, I go also. Our journeys have the same purpose and may well lie together, and perhaps I may help you in some of the difficulties of the road.'

At his words, her face shone for a moment with gratitude, then it suddenly paled. 'I will only be a drag, and my company will be the least safe in the world for you. I am already deep in your debt, and I cannot accept this service.'

'But if the lord be the Lord Lovat,' said Francis, 'if I have sworn to him that I would keep the Secretary from any such step though I followed him to the Tower, will this not change your decision?'

'But you said yourself that the errand was idle. How will you get a sight of him; and even if you see him, how will you bring him to a better mind?'

'I can but trust to chance to show me a way,' said he, speaking thoughts which had been with him on his road from the Highland glens. 'I do not value my life at overmuch, and for a desperate man there are many paths. But if the mischief is not done and he still lie unconfessed in the Tower, there is some hope; for a road may be found out of that place even for Mr Murray of Broughton.' Yet while he spoke he felt the futility of such a scheme – these two folk in a moorland house half a thousand miles from the capital, plotting a great state crime.

But to the lady it seemed a way out of all perplexities. 'We can do as Lady Nithsdaill did, as Anne Carew and Sir John Haltwhistle, and many others. Oh, what a thing is a bold man's mind! With you to help me I have hope, and I bless you from my heart, for it is most noble and generous to risk your life in my desperate cause. I cannot thank you, but God knows I shall ever remember.' And as cheek and brow flushed with her emotion, Francis for a moment sat lord and king in a crazy palace of cloud.

'We must not delay,' said she, 'for they will let no grass grow under their feet now they have got him. I have already made preparations for the journey, and I cannot see how two people should not travel quicker than a body of horse. There is my maid Anne who will follow me to the end of the world, and I will take a serving-man to see to the horses. You will find me the road, Mr Francis?'

Francis felt anew the desperation of the quest, but he had not the heart to throw obstacles in the way. This heroic lady might bid him steal the crown jewels, were her mind to be set at ease by such a deed.

'I accept the charge, my lady. God grant we meet with a happy fortune!'

'Nay, but I will have no "my Ladies" or "Mrs Murrays" or "madames",' she cried. 'Do you not see that the quest is ours, and we cannot enter upon it with a hedge of formalities between us? You have shown yourself a gallant gentleman, sir, and we set out on this journey as sister and brother. You will be Francis to me, and let me be Margaret, and then we shall be the better friends.' She spoke simply, but a blush rose to her cheek, and she played with the tassel of her chair.

Francis bowed, himself in turn violently out of composure. He rose and went to a window which looked over a courtyard to a long wooded valley. There was now no bustle in the place, no moving of horses, or running of serving-men. Only in a corner stood a great travelling-coach, which a single groom had washed and made ready. He was passing a brush over the panels.

The lady had come to his side, and looked on at the picture. He could not forbear to glance at her as she stood by his shoulder, so tall that her hair was but little below his cheek; and he noticed that her eye had filled as she gazed.

'What is the fellow doing?' he asked.

'He is doing my commands,' she said. 'Can you not see his work? He is painting out the arms of Murray from the panel, that no roadside passer may know them and witness the tragedy of an old house.'

He looked, and sure enough the man had all but obliterated any colour from the level black wood.

'It was a handsome coat as one might see in all the land,' she said softly, as if speaking to herself. 'First and fourth there was the old coat of Murray, three silver mullets on an azure chief with a black hunting-horn below on a silver field; second, it bore three silver fraises for the kinship to the house of Fraser; and third, the three gold cushions of the vanished house of Romanno. Did you know the motto and crest of Mr Secretary Murray, Francis? There it is; Robin is almost at it, and soon it will be no more. A dove with an olive branch, and *Pacis nuntia* for a device! Now I wonder what old raider chose that foolish text to set below his arms. I had never heard that the Murrays carried peace to men in their hearts, save – Ah, God help me! – that traitor's peace that one of the house is now seeking! A dove with an olive branch. Aye, it is suitable irony, and I praise the wit and foresight of the old cynic who first wrote it. At any rate it is all done with now, and I go out to the world without blazon or history. Heigho, I feel quit of a load, and yet I am melancholy today over the end of so long a story.'

Then Francis took his leave and went down to the village, where he found the landlord and held consultation; for much of Mrs Murray's own possessions were to be left in his charge against that seizure of the house which must soon follow. But the main point was the line of journey, and here he found a ready informant. For in the old days of the '15 this man had travelled far into the Midlands of England, and since then had gone many times to the South with droves of cattle. He drew up an itinerary as far as his knowledge permitted, and gave it into Francis' keeping, adding many prudent hints about lodging by the way and the least frequented paths. The honest fellow had much ado to speak clearly, for grief at the melancholy fortunes of his mistress choked his voice and confused his judgment. 'We hae a' our troubles in thae times,' he cried, 'but to see the sair end fa' on our puir feckless leddy is eneuch to wring tears frae a heidstane. The men are to bide canty at hame, but the women must up and awa to weir their herts on a desperate ploy. Lord, siccan days!'

When he returned to the house on some small errand it was already drawing towards evening. He found Margaret in the same west-looking room, fingering for the last time her treasures. 'I must carry little,' she said in answer to his look, 'for a burdenless rider gangs easily, as the folk say, so I am taking a last look at certain old things for which I have a sort of affection. Men sit loose in those matters, but we women are cumbered about with a host of memories, and must always have our trinkets.'

She placed some jewels in their case, and shutting it went towards a spinet which stood by the window. 'I used to play old tunes on it,' she said, 'for the amusement of my father when he tired of idleness in his latter days. It's a long farewell to my spinet as to all else, but I must play one last air before I shut it. Have you any favourite catch, Francis?'

Francis shook his head, for in truth he had little music in his soul save of the large rough-and-ready order.

'Then I will play you an old tune of the Cause, which loyal ladies have sung for many years and will doubtless sing for years to come, seeing that there is little hope of their dreams being fulfilled. It is called "Lady Keith's Lament", and the music was made by the King's own piper, who was a Macrimmon of the Macleods. It goes haltingly to a spinet, but you shall hear it.' And she played a wild melody, singing to it some such words as these:

> 'A' are gane, the gude, the kindly,
> Low in the moss and far on the sea,
> Men o' the North, men o' the muirlands,
> Brave to battle and laith to flee.
> I was aince a lady o' pride,
> High my hame abune the heather;
> Now my silken gown I tine,
> I maun fare in wind and weather.

'Kin and kith in weary battle
By stranger waters across the faem
Fell, and dying had mind o' sweet Argos,
The man of auld and the hills of hame.
The ship is rocking by the pier,
The hour draws nigh when we maun pairt.
Then fare thee weel, my loved, my dear,
Bide I canna, though breaks my hert.

'They are rude, simple verses,' she said, 'but to me they are
extraordinarily touching. There are other lines which tell of a
brighter hope.' And with some enthusiasm in her voice she
sang:

'But though I now maun wander dowie,
And drap the tear on cheek sae pale,
Yet shall our dule be turned to joy,
For God maun let the richt prevail.
My father was a guid lord's son,
My mither was an earl's daughter;
And I'll be Lady Keith again
The day the King comes ower the water.'

As she finished, she sat for a long time motionless, looking out
of the western windows. As for Francis, he fell into a like mood,
and neither spoke for long. The sight of this woman, young,
unfortunate, bright with a long-descended, subtle beauty, sitting
there singing a sad old ballad on that last day of calm before the
stormy morrow, moved him more than he could tell. Something
in the haunting notes of her voice, the sunset light on her hair,
and the long line of golden hill land which gleamed from the
window, seemed to him an epitome of all the fervours and
sorrows of life. He sat musing till she rose and shut the spinet.

'It is time to have done with old song, Francis. Henceforth it
is grimmer work for you and me.'

SEVENTEEN

A Journey to the South

From Broughton to Moffat is a short day's journey even for an old travelling coach, but the way is rough and grass grown up the narrow glen of Tweed to the high moors and the source of the Annan. Thence in a long day through pleasant Annandale you may come to the ridge of Esk and pass on to Carlisle walls. The two days were days of sunny, windless weather, and the clear air of the hilltops put an edge upon the travellers' spirits. Margaret seemed to forget her troubles, and after the way of woman, was interested in each passing face. As for Francis he had a heavier burden, but even he accepted the inevitable. He served the lady in a somewhat clumsy fashion, for he had no notion of the civilities of a fine society; but as the hours passed the two grew very excellent companions, while some spice of humour enlivened their sombre talk. For take any two clear and honest souls and set them in such a position; you will find them at first constrained and foolish, but as time goes on they will know each other for the human being that he or she may be, and look sanely into the future.

Carlisle was in an extraordinary stir, what with things political and the yearly summer fair. Daily batches of prisoners came South to these walls and soon many brave hearts sighed out their life from a tow on the Gallows Hill. Farmers from the hills were everywhere in the streets, drovers and shepherds thronged the ports; and each inn was filled with brown-faced bedlamites who made the night hideous with their din. In a little inn near the south gate, Francis found lodging; this much he had settled at Broughton, for the place was quiet, and the landlord no ill friend to the lost cause. There he left Margaret and her two servants, and went out to the streets in the late evening to ponder over the tangle of his affairs.

Money must soon be thought of, for his funds were already running low. He had no knowledge of the lady's wealth, but though she had been amply rich he would have died sooner than let her pay a single crown. When she came to Lady Manorwater's house his task would be ended; meantime she was his charge, the journey was by his advice, and he alone would see to the lawing. It was an old-faced, grim-looking man who stalked through the rabble of drovers in the darkening street.

Suddenly he brushed against one who stared full in his eyes. It was the face of an elderly, grizzled gentleman, clad in stout, simple country clothes, with a long jowl and deep eyebrows. Something in the air demanded recognition, and Francis involuntarily stopped. The man did likewise, and for a second the two blocked the causeway. Then like a flash came a happy intuition to Francis' brain. 'May I have a word with you, sir?' he asked.

The stranger nodded and led the way across the street to a little public, where he climbed a stair to a room above the causeway. The place was still yellow with sunset, and in a mirror on the wall Francis saw his own reflection. He almost cried aloud, for save for the twenty or thirty years' difference in age his was a double of his companion's face. His chance thought was now certainty.

'And now, sir, what is your business with me?' said the elder man.

'Why, my business is simple,' said Francis. 'I have come to claim kinship, sir. You, I think, are my uncle Robert?'

'So,' said the man solemnly. 'I jaloused as much the first glisk I got of ye. Ye will be Francie's son. Ye favour him, save that ye're sae muckle wiser-lookin' as ye seem less drunken. God, man, ye have the Birkenshaw glower maist uncannily in your een. Ye are the leevin' image o' my father. And what is it ye seek wi' me, nevoy Francis? Abune a', what brings ye to Carlisle toun in thae days o' war?'

'Listen to me,' said the other, 'and I will tell you a story.' And briefly he told of the last year, of his wanderings and his toils, and now of his final charge. The man heard him out with a grim face.

'Ye are like your kind, Francie, you and your trokings wi' outlawed Jaicobites. There was never a Birkenshaw afore took up wi' sic a bairnly cause.'

'I have heard bits o' the family history,' said Francis, 'but I never heard that it was the wont of our folk to leave a man when his back was at the wall or to refuse a woman aid.'

'Ye may put it that way if ye like,' said the man, 'but ye canna deny that it's unprofitable.'

'Then I leave that branch of the family's work to you, my dear uncle. I am content if I can keep a coat on my back. Has Markit paid well these last years?'

'Off and on,' grumbled the other. 'The land's ower unsettled for peaceable folk to dae guid business.'

'Because I am about to ask the loan of a hundred guineas,' said Francis boldly.

'A hundred guineas,' cried Mr Robert Birkenshaw. 'A hundred golden guineas! The man's mad! Heard ye ever the like o' sic a speiring! A hundred guineas, quotha! Mair like a hundred pence!'

'But you will give it me?' said Francis, 'seeing that a journey cannot be decently finished without gold.'

'But what's the need o' the journey, man? Gang back to Dysart to Gregor Shillinglaw and clerk awa among the writer lads like an honest man.'

'You know fine you would never have me do that,' said Francis. 'Is our house fallen so low as to neglect a plain duty for lack of gear?'

Mr Robert Birkenshaw presented a lamentable sight, his face red with emotion and twitching between love of his gold and the impulses of an honest heart. 'What can I dae?' he cried miserably. 'I'm no mean and I wad uphaud the family honour, but I'm dooms puir though folk ca' me rich.' Then with a splutter he took out a bag of gold from a flap-pocket and flung it on the table. 'Damn ye, Francie, tak it,' he cried. 'Tak it and use it weel. I've nae bairns, and whae's to lend to the family if it's no mysel'? Ye say ye are serving a leddy. Sit ye doon, and we'll drink to her if she's bonny. What's her name?'

At the mention of it the old pagan cried aloud in glee: 'I aince saw her, and she was as bonny as Queen Mary. Francie, lad, it's a guid errand ye're on, and I'll risk anither hundred if ye need it.' And so the lady's health was drunk and Francis sat on at the wine till late, hearing old fragments of family tales. So when at last he sought the inn, it was with some affection for his fellows and a more kindly outlook on life.

It would be dull to follow that hurried journey after the style of an itinerary, for it was monotonous and without interest save the casual variations of weather. Among the Westmorland hills the drought broke in a chain of storms which set every hill water roaring and made the fords hard for a carriage to pass. It was weary work both for Francis without on his horse, opposed to the buffeting of rain, and for Margaret and her maid within, who had no outlook but the dull streaks of water against the panes and a perpetual line of rough hill land. Sometimes it cleared towards evening, and then the lady would dismount and walk down the yellowing mountain track where the pools glowed in links of pure fire. In these hours she became cheerful, but in the long black showers she was sad and absent-minded, dwelling always on the past and its melancholy change. As for Francis, he was so old a wayfarer that he endured all weathers with equanimity. Only, when soaked to the skin and with no sight but blank hills, he would begin to think on the futility of his errand and torment his brain with projects of vain endeavour.

But with the lowlands came summer days when the sun was hot in the sky and the roads white underfoot. It was now that Margaret recovered her spirits and found humour in every halting-place and something pleasant to her curiosity in the vivid life of the road. Her cheeks got a touch of colour, till she no longer formed such a sharp contrast to the gipsy Francis. Yet the life had still all the hardships of a journey, for the roads were broken in many places with the recent passage of armies, the inns were filled with an air of suspicion, and piteous sights were always at hand to remind of war. This was in the North, but as they drew to the Midlands they found a lush and settled country which seemed terribly unfriendly to fugitives from a mourning land. For the first time they felt their presence among a people of alien sentiments and blood, a peaceable folk who dwelt among orderly hedgerows and neat, garden-like fields. And with the thought the bright and bitter past grew more irrevocable, and both alike were plagued with memories.

For Francis each day meant much careful forethought and not seldom high-handed intrusion. As it chanced, many of the inns were choked with the stream of travellers between North and South, and to get comfort he had to assume an air of dignity and show a bluff self-confidence he did not feel. Fortunately his purse was heavy, and in this easy land he found money a passport to more things than in the flinty North. But his mind was on a perpetual edge, for to haggle about the little things of life had never been his task before, and he found it irksome. His consolation lay in Margaret's immunity from such trivial cares; if her life must be sorrowful and vain, it would at least be free from the grossness of worry.

The road was uneventful though it was the morrow after a war, and one incident alone is worthy of record. In a little town on the Warwick borders they halted for a night, and after dusk Francis went out as his custom was to sober his thoughts with the night air. A year ago he had been a boy; now he felt himself an ageing, broken man, driven in curb along a stony path of virtue, a man passionate yet austere, with a cold, scrupulous heart and a head the prey of every vagrom fancy. A man with great capacities, truly, but scarcely a man to live pleasantly, at ease with himself and the world.

Round the gate of the inn-yard there was the usual idle throng. As he jostled his way through, one turned sharply round, recognition shining in his eyes. He put his hand on Francis' shoulder and followed him to the street. 'Mr Birkenshaw, my dear man,' he cried, 'do I trust my ain een? What brings ye here o' a' places on earth? I have had hell's luck since I left you at Leidburn, but you look stout and flourishing.'

When Francis recognized in the tattered lad the great Starkie, his former friend, his first feeling was of rage, fierce and unthinking. What right had this tatterdemalion, this ghost from the past, to come here and remind him of his folly, when he loathed it with his whole heart and soul? It was a pitiable figure, unshaven, haggard, with blear eyes and a shambling walk – a thing all but over the verge of beggary. And this had once claimed him as companion and now called him friend!

'Ye're the lad for me, Mr Birkenshaw. Ye've the master mind. I see ye've your braw leddy here that flyted on ye at Leidburn. Ye wad sune mak it up wi' her, for ye were the lad wi' weemen?' And he wandered into obscenity.

Francis took him by the collar and held him firm. 'See here, Mr Stark, if ye mention the lady's name again I will fling ye over the brig as I once flung ye into a ditch. You and me quitted partnership lang syne. If it's money ye want I will help ye to the best of my power, but let there be no talk of friendship.'

The boy whimpered. 'What's ta'en ye at an auld friend?' he cried.

'We have taken different roads, you and me,' said Francis.

'Ye may set yoursel' abune me if ye please. I am puir and you are rich, but I never took anither man's wife to traivel the highroads wi' me.'

Francis' fingers itched for his ears. 'I am not a patient man, as ye know, Mr Stark.'

'Patient or no, what do I care? But there's ae thing I can see wi' my een, and that is that there's some o' His Majesty's sodgers wad be glad to ken that ye were here and this leddy wi' ye.' He shrieked out his words while cunning twinkled in his little eyes.

'If ye say a word more, sir, or if ye dare but try what ye threaten, by God I'll send ye to your Master or ever ye can cheep. Do ye think I'm to be trifled wi' that ye try my hand here?' And he spoke so fiercely and with such angry eyes that the wretched Starkie seemed to shrivel up into apology.

'God, Francie!' he cried, 'gie me siller and let me off, for I'm starving.'

Francis thrust some coins into his dirty palm and watched him turn with scarcely a word of thanks and shuffle back to the inn. He was angry with himself, angry and ashamed. He pitied the wretch, and yet he loathed him and feared him and all the black past which he stood for. All his little self-composure was sent broadcast on the winds. He knew himself for the ragged, inconstant fool that he was, with but a thought dividing his veneer of virtue from the stark blackguardism of the vagrant. It was a stormy-souled man who tossed that night upon his bed, and rose in the morning with something greyer and bleaker in his determination.

As they passed out into the street a hollow-faced boy, still half tipsy from the night's debauch, cried good morning and a pleasant journey.

'Who is that man?' asked Margaret carelessly.

'He was one of my former friends,' said Francis, and rode forward.

As they came near the city where the roads from the north converged into one great highway, their journey was hindered with the constant passing of troops. Once more they were in the air of war, for a prisoner would pass, or a forlorn and anxious band of his kinsfolk, or a great northern lord or lady – all on their way to the centre of fate. Francis felt no fear of recognition, for his part, though played in the thick of affairs, had been secret from the multitude. Once only, when a lady whom he knew for Miss Cranstoun of Gair looked curiously at the tall, brown, sombre cavalier, did he turn away his face in doubt. But for the most part he held his head carelessly amid the throng of wayfarers.

The last night's halting-place was in a little town on the edge of Hertfordshire, a place among green meadows and rushy waters. At its one inn they found no one but a groom rubbing down a horse in the courtyard, and from the look of beast and man it seemed as if some person of importance were using the hostel. In the one dining-room when both sat down to supper a man was looking out of the window and drumming on the pane. He turned round at their entrance, and in a second Francis had in his mind the Highland inn and the carousing by the fire; for in the stranger he saw the lean face and heavy figure of Forbes of Culloden, the Lord President.

He felt he was recognized, he felt too that this man was well aware who was the lady who sat down with him. As it chanced, Margaret, who had seen the great lawyer scores of times, saw in him only a chance stranger; the dusk was gathering, she was tired with the day's toil, and she had no memory for faces. Forbes bowed to her curtly and without a word withdrew.

Francis ate his meal in a fever of anxiety. This man held both in his hands, and on the one former occasion of meeting he had insulted him, using as a weapon the name of this very lady. He knew of the popular report which made the Lord President's name a synonym for kindliness; but would he forgive so arch an offender, would he believe in the honesty of one who had so recently played a very different part? As soon as he could he left the room on some pretext to go in search of him.

He found him on the threshold, smoking with great deliberation and watching the glow of sunset over the fields. 'So we meet again, Mr Birkenshaw?' he observed dryly.

'It is on that point I have come to speak, my lord,' said Francis. 'You favour the other side in politics, but folk say that you are not a man that loves extremes. You see our wretched position, and I would ask your forbearance.'

'Ye are a Jacobite renegade,' said the other, 'and ye ask me to let ye be. That I can understand. But what for does this lady go with you? Are ye up to some new devilry, Mr Birkenshaw? For if ye are, lad, and would drag the bonniest woman in the land into the same bog, then by God I will make you pay for it with every bone in your body.' And his honest old eyes twinkled with wrath.

Then Francis with a shamefast air had to set to and tell him the history of the whole business, leaving out only such parts as concerned Lovat and the Prince. The man stopped him once and again, bidding him say no more about this or that matter, as it might be best for him to hear least. To the whole tale of Murray of Broughton he listened eagerly, murmuring under his breath. Then he took Francis' hand and stared hard into his eyes till he was fain to shut them against that steely glitter.

'I believe ye to be a true man, Mr Birkenshaw, and I ask your pardon. But this is a most lamentable tale ye have to tell me. Lord, man, I am driven crazy wi' the cruelties that are being perpetrated in the North on the puir people. I have run to and fro atween Stair and Tweeddale and got satisfaction nowhere. Aye, I have even licked the boots o' Cumberland, that haggis of a man, and suffered his clownish insults. I have been fleein' here and there night and day on the business of that fule Cromarty, and now I come up here to try once more and wring water out of a stane. Heard ye o' the death o' the two lords, Balmerino and Kilmarnock? God, there was a tale for history! And now there may be a third, if a' ye say is true, seeing that my Lord Lovat is taken.'

'Taken!' cried Francis; 'when, how?'

'I kenna,' said the other shortly. 'But a day syne a coach passed me and a great guard o' dragoons. I asked at the captain whae was his prisoner, and he bade me look inside; and there, grinning like a wull-cat, was the auld gross face o' the Fraser.'

EIGHTEEN

Of an Interview in an Unlikely Place

Lady Manorwater greeted her cousin with a frosty kindness. She was a pale woman of middle age, with the faded blue eyes and yellow hair of one type of Scotswoman. Fervently devout, as was the habit of her house, she carried her devotion beyond the other Catholic ladies of her time, and seemed ever posturing as a colourless saint. She thought of politics and her kinsfolk only as things far away; for her the living reality of life was found in the little chapel where at frequent hours she would retire to a dim world of candles and paternosters. Her two sons were boys in their early teens; and these with the servants made up the whole household in Great Marlow Street. A perpetual air of peril hung over the house, for men came there on short visits by day and night whose names had been proclaimed at law, and under the cloak of her pious and unworldly name treason had flourished and many a secret conclave had met undisturbed. She welcomed her cousin, for she had ever been fond of the beautiful girl; more, it pleased her that she should flee to her of all her kin at this hour of danger. It seemed like a recognition of that sanctity she believed to be hers.

Towards Francis she wore the stiffness which she used to all mankind. He was beyond the circle of her thoughts, unrelated by blood and alien in creed. The place was in no disorder; the life was as full of punctiliousness as in a great house in times of peace. At first it irritated Francis, for he who had come on solemn business had no inclination for a farce of comfort. But soon he was glad, for it distracted Margaret's thoughts and restored her to some portion of the elegancies of life. For her there was no going in and out and sharing in the gaieties of town. London was bitterly hostile to her cause; the streets were full of mobs shouting coarse party cries; and every day almost there was some fresh death for the populace to gape at. So the women abode indoors, while Francis wandered fiercely about the city.

As soon as he might, he sought out the lodging of the Lord President in the Haymarket. Forbes sat before a pile of papers, in a fine reek of tobacco smoke, while two harassed clerks scribbled in a corner. At the sight of the visitor he opened the door to a smaller sitting-room and bade him follow.

'Well, Mr Birkenshaw, how have ye been employing your time hereaways?' he asked.

'As best I could,' said Francis. 'This much I know, that Murray lies in the Tower with his honour still untarnished. Traitor or no, his treachery has not yet been put to proof.'

'True enough,' said Forbes. 'His examination begins next week. Have ye any work on hand ye may desire my help in?'

'It is my wish to get speech of the Secretary.'

Forbes hummed a little. 'It is unconstitutional,' he said, 'but it might be managed, though I see not what it will serve. Ye will be bearing him messages from his wife and kin?'

'I will be striving to bring him to a better mind,' said Francis. 'You know what I mean, my lord.'

'Pardon me, sir, I ken nothing but what I choose to ken. Besides, when so much is thrust down my throat there is no need for idle guesses'; and he looked up with a twinkle of intelligence which served the other's purpose.

There was silence for a little, while street cries floated up and a catch of a song which the Lord President whistled. 'I know the desperation of my plans,' said Francis; 'but then it is no time for little makeshifts.'

'If ye kenned the circumstances o' the time better, sir, ye might think them a little more desperate. Here are you, a lad without penetration, with no knowledge of the world, and ye are for visiting a noted prisoner of state and "bringing him to a better mind";' and the old man laughed sarcastically.

'I fight for my own hand,' said Francis gloomily; 'I can at least harm no man but myself.'

Forbes looked at him shrewdly for a second, and then drew his chair closer with a serious face.

'Would ye wonder greatly if I were to give ye some hint of the way the wind blows, Mr Francis? Would it amaze ye to hear that those in power are none so keen about this affair of the Secretary? His intention is over plain to mistake, and I can tell ye, sir, there are many on our side forbye myself that do not like it. The rising is utterly broken, and two great lords have already paid the penalty with their heads. It is a civilized people making war within itself, and the best statesmen have no craving for a glut of blood. Now mark ye what happens. The thing appears to be near a natural end. Scores of the common folk have swung for it, and there is hope that the worst is over. Then here comes the arch-plotter and gives himself up of his own free will. Any fool can make the inference. Mr Murray has something to tell, and there is but one person in our hands that such a tale can affect. This person, as it chances, is of great fame and far stricken in years. Ye follow my words, Mr Birkenshaw?'

Francis nodded.

'It is true that all the bloodhounds of the courts and the common ruck of the nation are never tired of butchery; but I speak of the great and wise who have the ordering of the land, and alone think truly of its welfare. Do you not perceive that this has some bearing on your case, sir?'

'Then I may hope—' began Francis eagerly.

'Softly, sir,' said the Lord President. 'I have nothing to do with what you hope. As an officer of law it is my business to see that you hope nothing. I was declaring a point of pure theory. Supposing, sir, supposing, I say, that the King's Government woke up tomorrow and found Mr Murray no longer a resident in a certain place, the best and most powerful would be the least sorry.'

'But the thing you speak of is near impossible.'

'Not so,' said the other. 'It would be possible – again I consider it in theory – for a powerful minister even to use some influence to see that the chance of the aforesaid gentleman's departure at least was there. The guard might be selected with some discretion on that particular night, Mr Francis.'

Francis was looking steadfastly at the floor, in a profound study.

'I think I have followed, my lord,' he said, looking up. 'I cannot tell you my gratitude.'

'There is a further matter to mention,' said Forbes. 'I presume that in such a supposed event a certain gentleman would fall into the hands of the law,' and he looked with meaning.

'It seems the only way,' said Francis.

'Then, of course, you have understood that the full rigour of the law's vengeance would fall on such a one. Whatever the Government might think in its private heart, it must show a severe front to the world. The lad that sought to fill Mr Secretary's place would swing from a tow ere the week was out.'

'I have considered it, my lord,' said Francis, though with a whitening face.

'Yet, supposing the lad to have a great spirit, he would deem his neck's safety a small thing compared with the honour of his friends?'

'Doubtless he would,' said Francis, between closed teeth.

At this the Lord President rose and gathered his papers together. 'I have to tell ye, sir,' he said gravely, 'that I honour ye for a very gallant gentleman.' Then, as he conducted him to the door of his lodging, he spoke quietly in his ear, 'I would recommend the third night from this if any one thought of putting the supposititious theory into practice.'

Hitherto a certain gentleman has come but little into our tale; now he must enter for an hour ere taking a long farewell. Times had changed with John Murray of Broughton, and it was a careworn, peevish man who sat in his prison chamber looking forth at the evening sky from a barred slit in the massive stone. He still wore the stained clothes he had travelled in, and what with the bare furnishing and the high, shadowy vaulting the scene and the man looked dismally comfortless. Most of his time he spent in pacing the length of his chamber, with knitted brow and lips that muttered ceaselessly. Toil had worn him thin; he had lost his florid colour; and what with his past privations and his present disquietude, it was a mere shade of his old self that sat moodily in the dusk of the evening.

Suddenly the door was opened by a turnkey and a visitor was ushered in. The warder left without locking the door, and the stranger advanced to his side. He had risen and stood inquiringly regarding a tall man, dressed plainly, and with a great horseman's jacket turned up about his ears. Not till he had advanced some paces to the light did he see clearly, and then he went forward to greet him with outstretched hands. For it was a mark of the Secretary that no name or face which he once heard or saw was ever forgotten.

'God bless you, Mr Birkenshaw, and I am blithe to get a sight of an old face. I am dying in these walls for some token that my friends have not forgotten me. But how comes it that you are admitted? for they keep me here as close as a mad tyke. I trust you have run into no grave personal risk on account of my worthless self?'

'It matters little how I came in, sir, and be assured I am running no risk. I have come to have some talk with you on a little private matter. But I would inquire after your health. How do you bear the mournful events of these latter days?' Francis spoke shortly but not uncivilly, for indeed the man's old rank and present discomfort impelled him to some politeness.

'Alas for a poor people!' cried the Secretary, sinking back in his chair. 'It is the way of all great causes, when brave hearts perish and senseless force crushes out loyalty and honour. You saw the saddest day in Scotland's history, unless there have been more awful crimes since I last saw the open sky.' He spoke in the style of Lovat, but to Francis, knowing the man shrewdly, the words seemed void of meaning.

'Many honest fellows have been swinging on Hairibee,' said he, 'and two great lords have met their doom on the Tower Hill.'

The Secretary shut his lips to hide their quivering. 'Even so,' he said, 'death is the end of all our desires. Did you bring any message from our friends in the North?'

'None,' said Francis, 'for my errand was but a matter of personal satisfaction. I came to ask if you fulfilled my request before the unhappy day at Culloden?' And he looked hard at the other.

'Why, yes,' said Murray simply. 'The letters have long perished. But what makes you so eager to ken?'

'The Lord Lovat is now in his enemies' hands,' said Francis, 'and, as there is like to be much brought against him, I wished to have no reflections that remissness of mine had brought him to his undoing. I do not hint anything of blame to you in the matter, but, if perchance the thing had been mislaid, it would be a formidable article in the charge.'

Murray ignored the slur and fastened on the mere statement, but it was clear that the words moved him.

'Lovat is taken, you say?' he cried. 'God, that is the end of the Cause with a vengeance, for they have gotten the greatest intellect in all Scotland or France. Have they brought him here?'

'It is some days since,' said Francis.

'But what can they prove against him?' he asked excitedly. 'He wasna out with the rest no more than Traquair and the Macleods. They're safe enough in their hidy-holes, and wherefore no Lovat? Ye say they will have much matter to bring against him, but it beats me to tell where they'll get a bodle's worth. I tell ye, sir, it will be a glorious acquittal.' And he looked on Francis with keen, sagacious little eyes.

To his hearer every word was offensive, so clearly did it argue a black purpose. No doubt the man acted his part cunningly, but there was a trip in his tongue, a falter in his readiness which belied him. Francis stared on him with gathering brows.

'And how is it with yourself, Mr Murray? Are you too to have a glorious acquittal, or are ye deep in the black books of the Government, like the honest gentlemen who are gone?'

The Secretary shook his head and passed his hand over his eyes.

'My days are numbered,' he said, 'numbered like the rest. I cannot look for mercy, for I have been at my master's side in all his calamities, and my name is near as well kenned as his own. Think you they will let me go now they have got me?' and even in his fright his breast seemed to swell with importance. 'I could have wished to die in my own land by the side of the brave Keppoch at Culloden or among the heather hills; but I have screwed my courage to the cauld death which awaits me. After all, it is but a short and easy passage to a better world.'

Francis sat in silence, his eyes scanning him up and down so intently that the voice quavered in the last words.

'It is of this chiefly that I came to speak,' he said. 'Your friends in the North, me among the rest, and many others whom it would not be well to name, have considered that you, as the Prince's best friend, would be a sore loss to the Cause. So by perilous ways we have contrived a means whereby you may escape and get safely over the water.'

Murray lifted his head, and looked with wild eyes upon the speaker.

'It's a device of little subtlety, but it has been used before with some success. You and I are much of a height. You have only to change clothes with me, wrap this same riding-cloak about your ears, and take your leave. I have purposely made the clothing somewhat kenspeckle, that the men may notice it and pay less heed to the face. The warders are picked men, and more than one are in the secret. At the last gate you will meet one of our own countrymen, an Argyll Campbell, who will give you the word, "To which passage?" You have but to answer, "To the Fords of Tyne," and he will follow you beyond the bounds, and see you safely to the door of your wife's lodging. There all is ready for flight this very evening, and ere morn you may be on the high seas. But you must hasten, Mr Murray, for the hours pass.'

But the Secretary's face showed no joyful surprise, no eagerness, only discomfort, timidity, and doubt. He rose stammering from his chair.

'I am grateful, Mr Birkenshaw, grateful to you and all the

good friends. Be sure I am grateful'; and he walked hastily up and down. 'But, my lad, it canna be. You purpose to stay in my place. Do ye not see that it means that your life will be forfeit, that you alone will be left to bear the wrath of a tricked Government? I may be soured and ill-grained, but God knows I have not come to such a depth as to allow such a cruel sacrifice. A young life,' he repeated. 'It canna be.'

'But I am willing,' cried Francis. 'Think what the thing involves. I am a landless, kinless man, and no one will mourn my end. Nay, it would be a matter of high satisfaction to myself that I could die so well. But you have a wife, you are a member of a great house; above all, you are one of the few props of a feeble cause.' Even as he spoke the words disgusted him. He saw treachery written so plainly on this man's face that he would have been glad to catch him by the neck and drive him out perforce. Something of his feelings must have been apparent, for Murray asked suddenly –

'Had Meg anything to do with this errand? It would be like one of her daft games.'

'Surely your wife has a hand in the matter,' said Francis, 'seeing that even now she is waiting to carry you with her to France.'

'I might have guessed it,' he said. 'But what sort of scheme is it? How could you think it so easy to win abroad when the seashore is watched by the King's dragoons like the Tower courtyard? It is mere madness, Mr Birkenshaw; I canna consent.'

Now in these last words the true reason of all lay apparent. He had some plan on hand which would bring him certain safety, and he had no mind to change this security for the difficult chance of a midnight flight. He was so stripped to the framework of his nature that Francis could read his thoughts in his eye, and at the sight the young man's blood ran hot with rage.

Then of his own accord Murray brought the farce to its close. He sat down squarely in his chair, and looked guilelessly at the other. 'You have my best thanks, but the thing is beyond my power. I cannot hold my safety, nay, even the safety of a great cause, dearer than my honour, and if I consented to your plan my conscience would never give me another moment's peace. I am no coward, sir, to fear death, and in waiting here I but await the doom of many of my own kinsmen and kindest friends.'

He stopped abruptly, for Francis stood over him, a fury of hate. 'My God, sir,' he cried, 'if you value your soul, stop this canting talk. I will tell you why you will not leave this place. You have some Judas secret to tell to our enemies which you hope may save your own coward neck and give you back your possessions. That is the hell's trick you would play, and may the Lord in heaven have pity on you, you lying dog, for I will have none.'

For a second the Secretary's life hung in the balance. The 'Birkenshaw glower,' once famed over Tweeddale, burned deep in the eyes of this young avenging fury. His fingers twitched at his sword's handle. The thought of slaying this man, and so putting an end to all the difficulty, had occurred to him once and again, and had always been put from him. Now it rose uppermost in his mind. The memory of a woman's tears drove him frantic, and Francis for one instant was on the verge of murder, while Murray lay back gasping in his chair.

But the white, weak, unwholesome face deterred him. The man seemed worn with toils, seemed spiritless, friendless, and feeble. He could not draw upon him any more than upon a woman. With a cry of despair he turned upon his heel and left the room.

At the last gate the Campbell hailed him. 'To what passage?' he asked.

'To the Fords –' said Francis mechanically, while the man made as if to join him. Then, recollecting himself, 'No, no, Heaven knows where,' he cried almost with tears, and hastened out into the darkness.

As Margaret sat watching by the window in a pitiful state of anxiety, Francis came roughly into the room. She ran swiftly forward and laid a hand on his arm, for such little tendernesses had been common in her ways of late.

'Why, you are back!' she cried, 'and I had never thought to see you again'; and with all her striving she could not keep a ring of exultation from her words.

'It is all lost, my lady,' said Francis hoarsely. 'I was a useless messenger. The Secretary has scruples about leaving his present quarters, and I was unable to persuade him bye them.' And with a foolish smile he laid his horseman's cloak on the table.

Margaret stood looking with sad, drooped eyes. 'Nevertheless you have done your most, Francis.'

But he was not listening. He had sat himself down before the table, and had leaned his head on both hands. 'Oh,' he cried, 'I have no gift of success. Whatever I take up miscarries. I am but a poor sort of fushionless creature, meant to be guided by stronger men. All that I do ends in moonshine. I can see no light in the whole black pit of this life.'

'Nay, Francis,' said she, 'surely there is some comfort, for you have tried nobly. I thank God you at any rate are left me.'

It was a foolish argument, but he, lifting his eyes carelessly at the words, saw something in the lady's face which made him redden and stare hard out of the window.

NINETEEN

The Last of the Secretary

Amid a crowd of notables and fashionables, where the wits of the coffee-houses rubbed elbows with the beaux of the Mall, Francis pressed to hear the last scene in the drama which had been played athwart his own life. The Lord President had gained him admission, and so this morning he stood in the great hushed Westminster chamber, watching the lords in their robes, the frowning bench of judges, and at the bar the huddled figure of the old lord with his two piercing eyes still mocking at the world.

It was a farce even to his layman's eye – a cruel, fantastic farce, with death waiting to pull down the curtain. Lovat had no aid but his own tongue, and for days he had toiled, cross-questioning witnesses on the other side, putting the necessary inquiries to his own supporters, till his face had grown ashen grey and he had swooned at the bar. His four counsel were of the most ineffectual cast, and would have turned the whole affair into an ugly mockery by catching at points of form but for the old man's restraining voice. At first he did his work well, even jocularly, but as his weariness grew greater his questions lost their pith and he relapsed into dignity and silence. The bearing of the old traitor struck Francis with admiration – at once deferential and free, defiant and courteous. He had his compliments for the lords, his tags of quotation, his excellent sentiments; but the certainty of death seemed to give a nobility to what had seemed before a farrago.

But as Francis listened and waited, the finishing touch was added to the picture; for into the witness-box came a shamefast figure, the very one he had held at his mercy in that Tower chamber, and to which he had shown a way of life it would have none of. Every eye in the assembly turned to those square feet of wood where the witness stood meekly, looking with conciliating eyes to the benches of lords and nervously fingering his cravat. Every face was eager with curiosity, some dark with ill-concealed disgust, while among the few friends of the prisoner there were twitching lips and hands hard at side.

Lovat had sunk in a stupor of weakness, and had not noticed the new arrival. Murray answered questions glibly and precisely in a tone of utmost cheerfulness. Then the clerk read the statement wherein he, John Murray, umquhile of Broughton, with the deepest penitence for past errors, with promise of amends and hope of His Majesty's infinite clemency, told to his gracious captors the full tale of the late lamentable events, more especially the part played by Simon Fraser, called the Lord Lovat, certain documents being adduced in proof of such statements. As the soft voice of the witness and then the hard clerk-like tones fell on his ear the old lord roused himself to interest. The shaggy head grew erect, and the eyes played with the unhappy man as he shifted his balance from one foot to the other and sought in all that place for a friendly glance. Ere the thing was finished he had hazarded a look at the man he had ruined and then drawn back in terror. He could not face the silent mockery of those eyes, the eyes of the wisest head in Scotland. Much they had seen, those eyes, at home and abroad, at the King's court and in the wild Stratherick. And now, with no fear of man, they looked through the one who had lent the chief hand to his overthrow.

The Lord High Steward asked if he would question the witness.

Lovat bowed politely. 'Nay, my lord,' he said, 'I think Mr Murray and I already understand each other'; and the smile on his lips was caught by the rest till Francis found himself all but laughing at the singular comedy.

The clerk rose according to custom, to read the portion of the defence which had been set in writing against Murray's charges. It was excellent rhetoric, stinging words under which the unfortunate gentleman cowered in some misery.

'Murray, the most abandoned of mankind,' ran the paper, 'who hath sought like another Catiline to patch up a broken fortune upon the ruin and distress of his native country; stealing into France to enter upon engagements upon, your Lordships may believe, the most sacred oaths of fidelity, and now appearing at your Lordships' bar to betray these very secrets, which he confessed he had drawn from the person he called his lord, his prince and master, under the greatest confidence.' So the clerk read, while the assembly grinned, and Lovat smacked his lips at his own invective.

Francis had no heart for more, but as he turned to push his way back, he caught a glimpse of the Lord President in the crowd. He also seemed about to leave, and the two met in the great corridor.

'This is the work of your friends,' said Francis wildly.

'It is the wark of my friends, and I am bitter ashamed. The fules! To set an auld man on a pinnacle to be mocked at till he gets him an appearance of virtue he never could have worn otherwise. I have been Sim Fraser's neist neighbour all my days, and though I could not help but like the man, I kenned him ower weel to trust him with a bodle. But I think shame to see him worried like a rabbit in a dyke, and him wi' his grey hairs. Be sure, Mr Birkenshaw, the Fraser will come out of the game with the maist credit.'

'I want a further favour, my lord,' said Francis, 'and it is that I be allowed to visit Lord Lovat before his end. There are some matters that I would like to talk over, and certain passages between us want redding up.'

Forbes knit his brows. 'It canna be till the trial's ower,' he said. 'They keep him ower close. But after – it is possible. Maybe you might win to him the last night.'

Francis thanked him and hurried out to the cheerful life of the street. The place was full of cries and the rattle of vehicles, the shouts of chairmen, and the hum of voices. It was a fresh, breathing world, and above was the infinite unchangeable blue of sky. For a second the cobwebs of intrigue were cleared from his brain. He saw the littleness of man's schemes, the ease of death, the cataclysm of hopes and fears, as in a sharp moment of time. But again he was back at his memories. Here in this alien place the last blow was being struck at a cause he had stood for. Tush! It was little he cared about the Cause, it was the people he had served and loved, the old memories and senti-ments of the few against the many, which were being swallowed up in this callous present.

For days he wandered fiercely in the streets, picking up frag-ments of news and cursing his powerlessness. He heard of the verdict, and then of the sentence of death received with a cheerful composure, even with a joke. At the hearing his old admiration revived for the indomitable man who could wait on the last enemy with a gibe. He counted the hours till the day of meeting. This, after all, was the fortunate warrior, who could go out of life with a twitch of his cloak and a word of scorn to his tormentors. The grossness, the cunning, the malice were all forgotten; he remembered only Lovat of the many generous sentiments, the great chief of Fraser, and the wisest brain in the North.

In the chill of the last Wednesday evening he was admitted at the gate of the Tower and led to the prisoner's chamber. As they went down the passage there were sounds of riotous mirth coming from the melancholy place. The warder looked bewil-dered. 'This is the way those wild Scots prepare for death,' he cried. 'I have had twenty-three honest gentlemen in my hands before they took their last walk, and all spent their last evening in meditation and prayer.' When the door was opened the room seemed filled with tobacco reek and the fumes of punch. Through the smoke Francis saw some few of Lovat's near kin, making as merry as if it were an alehouse in Inverness. General Williamson, the Lieutenant-Colonel of the Tower, sat opposite the prisoner, apparently in some discomfort. The old lord himself was reading from a paper, with a pair of enormous spectacles stuck on his nose and a handkerchief in his hand. A fire burned in the grate, but the prisoner's blood seemed chilly, for he wore enormous hose turned up over his knees and a pair of buckled slippers. His face had lost its pallor and shone with the heat and the wine.

'I am touched,' cried he, looking at the paper.

'Here's this body – Paynter they call him, a noble-hearted fellow for certain – writes to Mr Secretary Pelham, and I hear he has petitioned his Majesty likewise. And what do ye think the purport is? He wants the honour of being beheaded in the Lord Lovat's stead. See the creature fair fleeches and begs! "I pray you, sir, intercede with the King that the Lord Lovat may be pardoned." These are his words.' And he took off his spectacles, wiped them carefully, and then surveyed the company. 'I thank God that there are still good men in the world. "Greater love than this hath no man, that a man lay down his life for a friend." What think ye o' that, gentlemen?'

The Lieutenant said something about the man's being crazed.

'And indeed I am of your opinion,' said Lovat. 'Clearly the creature must be daft. For see what he calls me – "a vile traitor, an ungrateful wretch". Weel, weel, I doubt the poor gentleman is weary of living in this wicked world.'

Then, catching sight of Francis, 'Eh, here's a welcome face!' he cried, 'my ancient friend Francie come to bid the auld man guid e'en. Here's a seat by my side, lad,' and he pointed to a chair near the fireplace. 'Now, sir, this is a merry meeting, and, as we cannot reasonably drink to many mair, we will even drink to it as it stands.' And the Frasers filled up their glasses with due solemnity.

'Ye did weel, sir,' he said, speaking in Francis' ear. 'I have heard from Duncan Forbes of your efforts, and be sure I do not forget them. But, lad, I couldna jouk my fate, and I must e'en submit. I thought I got a glisk o' ye in the Hall some days syne. Did ye hear my defence that I had the clerk set to read? Was it no bonny, and was it no fine to see yon scunnering creature, Murray, shift about as I told the world what I kenned of him?'

Then he fell into a long strain of moralizing after his fashion, but the near approach of death gave a flavour to his words which exalted them almost to wisdom. 'See, Mr Birkenshaw,' he said simply, 'ye are a young man and may take a word of counsel.

I have maybe made a hash of my life, for I was ower wild and headstrong, and maybe ower given to the sins of the flesh. But after all I have had my sport out o't. I have had my fingers in every pie that's been making, and, faith, I have created some sort of a steer in the world. And that would ever be my counsel to young blood – to gang forrit, set the world in a bleeze if ye can, and if ye get your hair singit as I've got mine, ye need never heed for the sake o' the graund spectacle.'

He took out his watch and considered. 'Twelve hours more in this middenstead of a world,' he said, speaking loud to all. 'Now mind ye, Shamus Fraser,' and he turned to one of his friends, 'ye hear the last injunctions of your chief. Ye will have my body buried in the kirk of Kirkhill, for there lie all the generations of Lovat, and I've put a note in my will by which I leave bountith to all the pipers frae John o' Groat's to Edinburgh to play before my body. Lord, it will be a braw music, and I wish I could be there to hear it. But it's like that the Government will not allow it,' he said sadly. 'King Geordie is no sae mensefu' as King Jamie, and he has nae sense o' humour.' He looked at the embers for a little and then turned round more cheerfully. 'At any rate all the old women in my own country will cry the coronach, and it will be a wonderful crying, for I am the greatest chief in all the Highlands. And I will never see the heather hills more, nor the rigs o' Corryarrick'; and for a second his mocking face relaxed into plain sorrow.

'I drink a good journey to you, Macshimei,' and a tall Fraser rose with a trembling glass.

'Amen,' said Lovat, tossing off a cup, and then emptying his pipe ashes on the hearth. 'See, gentlemen, the end of human life is like this snuff o' tobacco. A moment we are bleezing finely, and then we go out and nothing is left but grey ashes.' And he sighed and sat for a little with his head on his breast.

He turned to the Lieutenant and asked to see his little daughter. 'Where's the wee bairn that used to come in and play hunt-the-gowk wi' me? She'll no be in bed yet, and I would like to bid farewell to her. She was a fine bit lass.'

'I fear, my lord, you cannot see her,' said the man huskily. 'She has done nothing but weep for two days since ever she heard of your fate. She is a little traitor at heart, for she abuses the King and his judges most roundly. I heard her only yesterday designing an escape for you from prison such as was given to the Apostles at Philippi. She will miss her playfellow most bitterly.'

'Will she indeed?' said the old lord. 'God bless the dear child, and make her eternally happy, for she is a good, kind-hearted lass.'

Shortly after this he desired that all should leave him save Francis and the Lieutenant. When they were alone he asked the latter to fetch Mr Baker, the chaplain of the Sardinian ambassador, to give him the last comforts of the Church. 'But I had thought you a Presbyterian, my lord,' said the Lieutenant. 'You passed for such through most of your career.'

'Policy often makes havoc wi' a man's creed,' said Lovat, smiling wickedly, 'but I have ever abode in the faith of the only true Kirk. I adhere to the rock on which Christ built His gospel. I ground my faith upon St Peter and the succession of pastors from him down to the present, and I reject and renounce all sects and communities that are rejected by the Kirk. That is my confession of faith, and if you think it of sufficient importance in the world, sir, I will put it down in writing.'

'I did not know you were a theologian,' said the other, in some wonder.

'The world little kens what I am,' said Lovat, and it was hard to tell whether the whole thing was jest or earnest. 'Some day mayhap the world will do me justice, and the little children of the clan will be proud to think of their chief. But I've been like the Almighty, hiding my ways in the sea and my paths in the great waters, and it will take a wise man and a cunning to find them out. Francis, you have seen much of me, and I might have looked to you for a proper understanding of me, if ye hadna been so thick in the heid and dour in your ain conceit.'

'I have one question, my lord,' said Francis. 'I have bungled the trust you laid on me, but I have striven to keep my word. Do you absolve me from any blame in your death? It would let me lie down with an easier heart.'

'Absolve ye, lad? Freely; and mair, I have to thank ye kindly. I bid ye goodbye, for there'll be little time the morn. Gang back to your ain land, lad, and take my blessing with ye. And now I must ask ye to leave me to myself for a little, that I may prepare for the putting away of mortality.'

'But, my lord,' cried the Lieutenant, 'I have heard that there are differences even within your creed. The Sardinian chaplain has the name of a rank Jesuit. Are you too of that persuasion?'

'A Jesuit?' said Lovat, with a twinkling eye and a gesture of doubt. 'Faith, no, when I think upon it, I am a Jansenist. But anything in the shape o' a priest will serve my turn. Goodnight to ye, gentlemen.' And with this last piece of mystification he bade them farewell.

TWENTY

The Death of the Lord Lovat

The morning was mist and rain with a wind blowing from the east up the packed streets. It was like a fête day in the town with people in Sunday clothes hastening Tower-wards. When Francis came down to the dining-room, a maid was scrubbing the hearth, the windows were open, and in the raw early chill there came a babble as of a city in expectation. He had slept scarcely a wink, being full of a kind of bitter excitement. For him the world at the moment held but one event and one man, and at the thought rage, compassion, and regret made a medley of his feelings.

Margaret appeared wrapped up in a thick cloak against the rawness of the morning. She wore the heavy veil she had thought needful for the open streets, and all her garments were of the sombrest black.

'I could not go dressed otherwise,' she said. 'I could not put on a fine gown to witness the death of a friend. My cousin tells me to stay at home, for I shall only break my heart to no purpose; but when so few of his countrywomen will be near, I should think shame to be absent.'

Tales of Lovat's deeds and last dying confession had been printed in flying sheets, and were hawked up and down the causeways. The crush was already setting eastward, and one man was telling to another his version of this great affair. The name of the terrible outlawed monster had been long in the people's ears, and now they were to have a sight of him in all the pomp and contumely of a traitor's death. From the hanging windows crowds of fine ladies had dared the morning air to look down upon the throng; some even had risen early and in their coaches sought a stand upon Tower Hill.

The cheerful holiday crowd brought tears to Margaret's eyes, as Francis with his great shoulders clove a way through, his dark, uncommon face bringing him a certain respect.

'We are strangers in a strange place,' she said sadly. 'What do these folk care for our broken King and people? And yet they say he had many well-wishers in this city.'

At Temple Bar the shrivelled heads of the Lords Balmerino and Kilmarnock grimaced at the crowd. At the sight Margaret clung closer to his arm. The rousing tale of Balmerino's conduct on the scaffold had stirred even the most Whiggish blood, and she looked at the poor dumb mouth, her face blanched with excitement, as in the old days when she had sat on horseback watching the entrance of the Camerons.

'But he was young and strong,' she cried, 'and he might well face death courageously. But my Lord Lovat is old and feeble, and he cannot stand squarely against his foes.' Then with a catching of the breath she would have stopped. 'Oh, it is horrible! And this is the issue of great expectations!'

The whole hill was black with folk and on stands were many more of the better sort all agape for the spectacle. The two halted yards off at the verge of the dense throng, where some carriages stood waiting. Afar like a toy building stood the scaffold with its bare timbers and the black-draped block and the guarded alley leading thither from the Tower gate. The thought of this one man alone or all but alone in that vast hostile sea of faces stirred Francis wildly, and he could scarcely bide still. The same thought was in Margaret's mind, for she looked with piteous eyes at the thick wall of men. 'Oh, that we could get near him,' she cried, 'that he might have kind faces to look upon at the end!'

As Francis looked round he saw in a coach among the others the Lord President. At once he made his way to his side. 'May I beg you, my lord,' he cried, 'to watch over this lady and take her home when all is over? I would fain get near Lovat today.'

Forbes glanced at the slim, beautiful figure. 'With all my heart, Mr Birkenshaw,' he said, while he held out a hand to

Margaret. 'The lady will see the last of our poor friend as well here as elsewhere. I wish you God-speed on your errand.'

'I shall win to him, though the crowd were ten times greater.' And in a second he was lost in the thick of men.

For many minutes he struggled as only the desperate can, elbowing fiercely, being struck again and again, gripping his opponents and half suffocating them, till he had forced his way past. Now and then he would come to a knuckle of rising ground whence he saw the scaffold, and always he noted gladly that it was empty. Weaker men were fainting all about him, but his supple vigour had its effect, and soon he was halfway through, and then only a quarter of the space was left. He was breathless, hatless, his coat torn in many places, and his face sorely scratched. Then, as he saw the wooden planks almost within reach, he heard a great sigh of expectation go through the multitude, and the tramp of men above the other din told him that Lovat was coming.

As he stood panting in the dense throng below, Lovat stood above him and cast a curious glance round the assembly. It happened on Francis, and his eager eyes told their tale. 'I pray you, sir,' he asked the Sergeant, 'to allow this young gentleman to come up beside me. He is a dear friend, and has but newly arrived.' The Sergeant, willing to pleasure the old man, gave an order, the crowd was opened by soldiers, and Francis found the way clear for him to ascend the platform. In a moment he was by Lovat's side.

Around – apparently for miles – was a dim circle of faces, and a hum rose from them, silent though they were, like the breathing of a great wild beast. Now and again a woman's or a boy's scream would break the air, only to be hushed in the pitiless mass. It was as if one stood on a pinnacle, watched by a million hungry eyes which bit into the soul. Lovat cowered for a second, for no feeling is more awful for the moment than to be one against a host; then his spirit came back to him, and he turned to Francis, smiling.

'The last time I stood before men under the sky was at my ain

Castle Dounie,' he said, 'when I heartened my folk to die for the Prince. I am like to need all the heartening myself now.' Then a twinge took him, and he all but fell into Francis' arms, while his clansman, Shamus Fraser, ran forward to help him. Supported thus, he limped across the platform, making a strange clatter in the quiet.

Suddenly in the midst of the crowd something horrible happened; for the scaffolding of a stand gave way, and the erection with its inmates fell on the packed array of heads. In a moment there was a wild panic, to which soldiers fought their way with difficulty. For a little it seemed as if a great catastrophe impended, for several men were taken up dead and mangled, and the crowd was all but hysterical. Then slowly the tumult subsided, the dead were borne out, and eyes turned again to the scaffold.

Lovat had watched the scene with delight.

'There's some o' them killed,' he whispered breathlessly. 'Weel, weel, so be it. The mair mischief the better sport.' Francis looked at him in amazement. A second ago he had been ready to venerate this man as a hero; now, behold, it was the old Lovat back again, a very malicious, jeering hero, laughing cruelly in the article of death.

'The sport's bye,' he said, as expectant silence reigned again, 'and it's my turn to divert my friends. It's as weel, Francis, that it's an easy job, demanding small exertion on my part, for I am a done auld man.'

His whole humour seemed to change, as if he felt that men expected something high and heroical in his final bearing. He gave one last glance at the crowd. 'God save us,' he cried, 'why should there be such a bustle about taking off an auld grey head that canna get up two steps without two men to support it? Francie, your airm, my son!'

He limped up to the block, nodded cheerfully to the executioner, and begged to see the axe. 'It might be sharper,' he said, 'but it hasna far to gang, and will maybe do.' Then taking his gold-headed cane, he cried to a young lad who stood weeping behind him, 'Alastair, my dear lad, take my staff and keep it weel for my sake. Ye've been a kind callant, and I wish I had a better gift.' The poor boy took it, crying very bitterly, and turned away his face.

Then taking off his coat and cravat with Francis' aid, he laid them down carefully, bidding the executioner keep them if he cared. Beside the block stood his coffin, and stooping down he read the inscription. '*Simon Dominus Fraser de Lovat,*' he read, '*decollat . œttat . suœ 80.*' For some seconds he continued gazing, and then turned away with a sigh. 'Happily my fame does not rest on this short line, Francis,' he said. 'But, indeed, what am I thinking of?' and he declaimed:

> '"*Nam genus et proavos, et quae non fecimus ipsi,*
> *Vix ea nostra voco.*"'

He turned to Shamus Fraser, and taking both hands bade him farewell. 'My dear Shamus,' he cried, 'I am going to heaven, but you must continue to crawl a little longer in this evil world.' And then he spoke to him shortly of his dying bequests, and his messages to his kinsfolk. The man was white and speechless, his dark face working with suppressed tears.

Meantime Francis was in no better plight. He had been with this man in fair and foul, he knew his innumerable vices, his treachery, his selfishness, and yet in this last moment he could look on him only as a heroic gentleman. On the scaffold in the midst of the waiting crowd he lived again the days in the hot heather, the fury of the lost battle, and the whole tale of his undoing; and always for a centre was the figure of this man with whom his toils had been shared. It was a quivering hand that took Lovat's wrinkled palm, and his lips were drawn to a thin line.

'And you, Francis,' said the old lord, 'What shall I say to you? Ye have been more than a son to me, and, O lad, I wish ye had been Master o'Lovat, and we two would have set a different face upon the business. Ye have the blessing of an auld man, my dear lad, and may you live long and die happy and be kindly treated as you have been kind to me.'

And then with great deliberation he turned to the block, and looking over the throng uttered the well-worn line, the last in the mouth of the hopeless:

' "*Dulce et decorum est pro patria mori.*" '

The next moment he had kneeled down, and ere Francis could look clearly the axe had fallen, and the head lay in the basket.

As, with brain in a ferment and eyes hot with unshed tears, he staggered from the platform, he heard in the hushed silence the voice of the headsman crying, 'This is the head of a traitor!'

With head lowered like a mad animal, Francis pushed his way through the choking streets. Some turned to stare at him, but his speed was so great that he left no time for more than a glance. A great impulse was on him to run to the ends of the earth till the madness of his physical strength and burning heart should be quelled. He comprehended the joys of battle; he would have gloried in that hour to stand with his back to the wall against a multitude. One insulted citizen gripped him by the arm as if to demand some apology for jostling; but before he knew the man was sitting in the gutter and Francis was many yards down the street. And all the while there was the cold of rain about him and a wind which blew grateful on his forehead. He was going out into the earth, kinless, purposeless; yet a man who had once lived and dared.

When he came to his lodging, he found Margaret sunk motionless in a chair in her outdoor clothes, her eyes fixed vacantly on the leaping fire. She rose quickly with burning cheeks at his entrance.

'Oh, tell me all! I saw nothing save the horrid deed. How did my lord bear himself at the end?'

Then Francis told her the whole tale, marvelling the while at his excitement. His voice rose high ere he had done, and with unconscious art he pictured the old lion in the midst of the crowd dying with a brave word on his lips. He told of the last greetings and the message to his kinsfolk. And all the while Margaret stood twining her hands, tears shining in her eyes.

'It was great, it was the death of a hero. Oh, God send we all show as brave a face to death. My heart has been bursting with rage all day, Francis, and yet I am half crazy with joy. We have not failed, though the Cause is lost and the Prince an exile, for we have shown a poor-spirited people how gentlemen may die. I shall pray ever for the soul of the Lord Lovat and the true men who have fallen. *Dona æternam quietem, Domine,*' and as the soft Latin fell from her lips, her wearied nerves failed her, and she fled sobbing like a child.

TWENTY-ONE

The Temptation of Mr Francis

That night there was little sleep for Francis. The figures and deeds of the day formed a long procession through his brain. He felt again in all their acuteness the emotions which had branded his soul. The truth is that the man was tired to death, what with physical labour and the more wearing toil of spirit. He was no more the sober, passionless man, but a tempest-tossed, sorely battered creature who had been strung to a pitch of high excitement, and was now sinking to a dull recoil.

But when he got some quiet from such vain dreaming, he set himself to shape out the future. It stretched grey and level before him, featureless, even now unalterable. There was but one thing for him to do. For the last year he had been striving desperately towards virtue. Now he must return to the writer's office and his old evil reputation. He must go back to Dysart and settle there as the solid man of law, and try to work out for himself a position of respect. There must be no more quixotry, no thought of mad capers in wars oversea. He must shape out his salvation in the place he had been called to, and settle to a life of loneliness cut off for ever from the past.

The thought was bleak, but he never wavered, for the man had true steel and fire in his soul, and had the daring to face an age of melancholy and routine, and he too in years but at the threshold of life. There seemed even some grim humour in it all. That he who had been a firebrand, all but an outlaw, should go back to the common task, was an irony for the gods to laugh at.

But this outlook of his own was but a little matter; there remained the graver question of the woman whose path fate had joined with his. He had seen how day by day her eyes sought his with a growing confusion; even in his blindness he had felt that this lady had come to regard all things as less than a word of his mouth. He stood to her as a hero, girt with the purple and fine gold of her fancy; he was the embodied Cause for which she had striven; and now at the turning of the ways there must come a day of reckoning. Her love was his for the accepting – she the great lady, with that delicate beauty and spirit; and for a second his heart beat exultantly. But the thought was banished, scarcely even with regret. For this man had outgrown temptation, and now this subtlest failed to touch him. He had but to join his life with hers, to go abroad and push his fortunes; it was a dazzling career which gleamed in the avenues of the future. Yet the renunciation cost him little, for with all his fire his nature was cold to the commoner human affections. He was returning to the vulgarity of home; and always in his mind would remain the image of the woman he had once toiled for. But to be with her always, to bring her into the glare of common day and the pettiness of household life – he had no heart for such degradation. In his soul he knew that each was better apart, living for the other's memory, fighting the battle with the other's name on the lips. But for aught else he was cold and careless; for his nature was capable of the heroical virtues, but unfit for the little moralities. He was ever in revolt from the domestic, the eternal wanderer in the ways of the world.

Lady Manorwater alone came to breakfast the next morning. He had always been a little in fear of this austere virginal woman who carried devotion writ on her face. She had an air of the monastic which seemed strange to the prosaic Francis. But now she talked gravely and kindly.

'It is time for my cousin Margaret to make up her mind, Mr Birkenshaw. I have tried to induce her to bide with me, but she cannot bear the thought of this land longer and declares she must go abroad. She is of my religion, but I have never tried to influence her plans. But she declares for a convent now. She would devote her life to God after the many sorrows she has faced in this world; and I have not tried to persuade her otherwise, for it would give her the days of rest which only He can give to the weary.'

'Where would she go?' he asked.

'I have already thought of that. I know well the Abbess at the little convent of Ste Thérèse by Arras. For my sake she would gladly receive the poor child and tend her like a mother. It will vex me sore to part with Margaret, but I cannot grudge her to God. And she will be happy if they can be happy who dwell in quiet and purity.'

'And I too must be going,' said Francis.

'And where?' said Lady Manorwater.

'I go North again, back to my own people.'

'But why?' she said. 'You are young and stirring. Is there not a better field for you than that sad and bloodstained land? A word, and I can get you service abroad, where you would find a chance for a man's work.'

'It cannot be,' said Francis resolutely. 'I thank your ladyship, but I have some faults to amend and some restitution to make before I can be at peace with myself. Forbye, I am but a pedestrian nature after all, and cannot easily get old things out of my mind. I must bide in my own land, for I cannot flee from myself, and to go to the foreign wars would be to try to forget a sore heart in the hurry of battle.'

Later in the forenoon a servant brought him word that his mistress wished to speak with him. He found her in the library, where above the fireplace the three lions' heads of Manorwater were cut deep in the oak. She was standing by the window, and her face seemed pale above her dark gown.

'Good morning, Francis,' she said. 'I was so weary with yesterday that I was late of rising this morning. Our work is over now, my friend, so we can take a rest.'

'I have heard of your plans,' he said. 'Your cousin has told me that you go to France to a convent. And I too am about to go, so it is time for goodbyes.'

She bit her lips at the words, and her voice had a quaver. 'These months have tired me so that I long for quiet to think and remember. Now that my work is done and all that I have lived for made hopeless, you cannot wonder that I wish for peace.'

Francis listened with bowed head. 'You can do no wrong, Margaret,' he said.

'And you?' she said suddenly; 'what will you do?'

'I go back to where I came from.'

'Oh, never,' she cried. 'It cannot be, it is too hideous and cruel. You might hew your way to fortune wherever you pleased. There is need of a strong man all over the earth, and you are strong and sure.'

He did not speak, but the words were very bitter to him.

Then she turned round till she looked full in his eyes.

'You cannot mean it?' she said. 'Ah, mercy! we have shared too many hopes together, we cannot part thus and go each our way into the bleak unknown. I was never fit for a life of piety, and you are too strong for a narrow fate. Oh, take me, Francis, and let us go away together. I am too noble a woman for God, it is a sacrifice which the Blessed Virgin herself could not bear to look upon. I know that I am speaking of sin, but what matters sin if we both can share it? Why, we might yet change the woeful fate of this land if we worked together.'

In a deep-set mirror on the wall she caught a glimpse of her face.

'See, dear,' she said, 'I am near as tall as you,' and she smiled tremulously. 'We are a handsome pair, and we will yet make great men bow to us.' And she laid her cheek on his shoulder.

'You are not angry with me?' she cried. 'I know I am wicked, but I cannot help it. I cannot part from you, and what are old foolish ties to a woman's love? Oh my dear, take me and let us face fortune hand in hand.'

Francis held her wrists very gently and looked into her eyes.

'Nay,' he said, 'you know better than I that this cannot be. Long ago you gave me a hand to raise me out of the mire, and I cannot have you be false to yourself. Be sure that I shall ever have you in my mind as the best and bravest woman God ever made. But we have each our own ways to take, and one cannot fight the battle better by beginning it with a folly. Marriage and love are for the peaceable settled folk, but you and I are not of their order. For good or ill we are on the open road of life, and we cannot turn back or aside.'

Margaret covered her face with her hands when he let her go, and her bosom heaved with sobbing. Then she lay back in a deep chair with closed eyelids.

'I am so weary,' she said, 'and, oh, I am so foolish. You are right, Francis, and God forgive me for my weakness. But we cannot forget each other, and there in that foreign place my thoughts will always be of you and the lost days. It is near the time for farewells, dear. Kiss me, that I may have something to remember, for I am sure that no other woman's lips will ever touch you.'

With bursting heart he leaned over her, and for an instant the long white arms were about his neck. Then she let him go, and he stumbled from the room.

That evening the house was unwontedly gay, for some few Jacobite gentlemen had been bidden to supper, and the friends of the Manorwaters had come to bid goodbyes before the journey into France. After the fashion of the broken party they allowed no sign of melancholy to appear, and the scene was as gay as if the time had been happy alike for all. Francis was in no mood for any meeting with others, but he could not in grace refuse to appear. In a little he was glad, for it comforted him to see how the end of the drama was played with spirit. As he watched the brave sight he felt how little a thing is failure in act if the heart be unbroken.

But the vision of Margaret fairly surprised him. She had dressed herself in her gayest gown, putting on her old jewels which had lain untouched for months. Like a girl at the dawning of life she moved among the guests, cheerful, witty, incomparably fresh and lovely. Once again she was the *grande dame* who had guided the Prince's councils and the honest gentlemen who stood for his Cause. For a second, he felt an overpowering, jealous craving for this woman, a repugnance to the greyness of his lot. And then it passed, and he could look on her and be thankful for this final spirit. It was the last brave flickering of life before the ageless quiet of her destiny.

TWENTY-TWO

A Long Leave-taking

The way lay over grassy ridges of hill and then at intervals among the bracken and boles of a great wood. The mist of the morning lay on all the far distances, and one might guess that behind the veil lay a wild and tangled land, that the slope did not stop a little beyond the edge of the haze but rose sheer into precipitous crags. It might have been Scotland, and as the coach rumbled down the highway Margaret when she looked to right and left saw a glimpse of a landscape now for ever lost to her.

To Francis, who rode as before at her side, the same notion kept recurring. It was the air and look of a northern glen, here in this soft English south country. He noted Margaret's abstraction.

'I am looking my last at a sight I love dearly,' she said. 'Oh, is not that cold, misty place like the kind country I have left? I can almost smell the heather and the fir wood at Broughton. You are happy, Francis, in your lot, for you will always be at home, and sleep at the end among kind folk.'

Slowly the land changed till by the afternoon they were on the seaward slopes and caught afar the long sweep of waters. In front rose the spires of the little fishing town whence they were to sail, and on the red roofs the evening light fell in a burning haze.

Amid the bustle of departure on the quay Margaret was left unnoticed. She stood apart, under the sea-wall, looking wistfully to the waters.

'There is a text from the Scriptures running in my head,' she said. 'Some one of the prophets wrote it. It is, "Weep not for the dead, neither bemoan him; but weep sore for him that goeth away, for he shall return no more nor see his native country." My life is ended, Francis, for all my joy has perished.'

'Nay, my dear lady,' he said, with something rising in his throat, 'you will have many happy days, and you will forget old sorrows. These last years have been but a little confusion of moorland wars, fought in the wind and rain by a poor people. You will soon cease to think of them and wonder at your present grief.'

'Do you think so?' she said sadly. 'I fear it will be very different with me. It is not the way of our exiles to forget easily. Nay, rather they fight all their battles with the old words in their hearts, and at the last, why, as my song says, they "fall, and dying have mind of sweet Argos".'

Then she turned abruptly.

'How long will you take to be back in the North?'

'A matter of weeks,' he said, 'for it will be done on foot. I am a poor man once more, and shall sell my horse before I start.'

'And what will you do then?'

'Seek a place in Mr Shillinglaw's office and give my mind to my work.'

'And after that?'

'Why, I shall grow old, like all men, and wander about the doors. Then death will come with a kindly face and I shall bid goodbye to the world – perchance to find a better.'

She smiled as if at the moment she saw the whole comic littleness of life.

'Our ways are not so different. After the colours the sober grey, for you as well as for me, Francis.'

Lady Manorwater was already aboard, and Margaret followed. The cables were slipped, and soon with creaking of cordage and a flapping of canvas the vessel stood out from the quay. Slowly the faces grew less, till a mere blur of white marked where Margaret stood by the ship's side. A kerchief fluttered for a moment and he answered, and soon only a speck remained in the circle of sea.

He stood at the far end of the quay, one foot on a broken stone, watching the sails melt into the evening. The salt fresh smell of the air was growing rawer with the advent of night; the once shimmering waters were sobbing below the piles; and afar to east and west a leaden dullness crept over the waves. But to the south there was still a track of light, and suddenly, clear and sharp, rose the vessel's outline against the rising dusk. In a second it was no more, and over the whole sky was rolled the curtain of evening.

But the man stood still till the last light had gone and the mist came up from the sea.

TWENTY-THREE

In the Nature of a Postscript

The patient scribe who has chronicled this tale has employed his leisure in seeking for further news of the two who figure chiefly. Nor has his zeal been unrewarded. Among the Manorwater family papers he had access to the letters of that Countess of Manorwater who when left a young widow married the Duke of Sanctamund, and cut something of a figure in the Regency days. Her ladyship was famous for her wit and her odd prettiness. She was of the school of Sensibility, and, it is recorded, made pilgrimages to the grave of Rousseau. She was famed too in polite circles in Paris in the early days after the Revolution, and through her kinship to the De Noailles claimed all the virtues of the old régime. But in the midst of her gossipy epistles there is one little letter in which she tells her friend, Emily Norton, of a visit to Arras and an hour spent in the grave-yard of the convent of Ste Thérèse.

'... Yesterday, ma chère, was a heavenly day, blue with white clouds sailing above, and all the place green with the tender spring of this climate. I found the graveyard, which is hidden away among cloistral grey walls, but kept trim by the piety of the sisters. After much searching I came on a little stone, much grown about with white roses, and on it the simple letter M, and the words, *"Pro sua patria"*. It was indeed the tomb of my unfortunate kinswoman. I confess, my dear Emily, that I could not look on it without a tear. Here in this green place lay my brave Margaret – *la Marguerite des Marguerites* – whose name as a little girl I used to worship. People say she went far from the paths of

virtue, that she used her beauty and her talents unscrupu-
lously for a foolish cause, but I cannot believe it. Here the
memory of her gentleness and goodness is still fresh, and
the old sisters have much to tell of *la belle Ecossaise*. Well-
a-day, we cannot judge; at any rate she has got peace; and
I confess I wept to think that even in her death she
remembered her own land and asked that the white
Jacobite rose might be set above her grave. I fear I can
write no more at present. The emotions of the day have
discomposed me, and I go to bed. In three days we return
to England, and till then with eternal love believe me your
ever-affectionate

VICTORIA MANORWATER.'

On the other hand the writer has searched the excellent series
of monographs on the Fife burghs for traces of Mr Francis.
There he was unsuccessful, but in a series of papers contrib-
uted by a former provost of Dysart to that most enterprising
sheet, *The Fife Journal and Herald of the Kingdom*, and composed
from the town papers, he has found something of interest.

'. . . In our list of talented townsmen of a former time,
none should be more highly esteemed than Francis
Birkenshaw, who succeeded John Henryson as Provost of
the burgh. He was a writer, having succeeded to the business of Gregor Shillinglaw (for whom see last number).
There were always queer stories in the town anent him,
for he was a wild lad in his youth and disappeared unac-
countably during the Rebellion, returning much graver
and wiser, which gave colour to a belief that he had seen
service with one or the other side. Nevertheless, he soon
acquired a responsible position in the place, and as head
of a flourishing business, was elected Provost in the year
1765. He introduced many reforms, particularly a system
of town pumps where the burgesses could get clear water,
their former source having been invaded by the sea. His

portrait hangs in the Town-house, and shows a grey-haired, hard-faced man, with cold, unfriendly-looking eyes. This indeed seems to have been his character, for he rarely graced the social board, but lived unmarried and utterly by himself, finding all his interest in his work and the town's affairs. He died at the early age of fifty-two, leaving his business to his head clerk, and his fortune – which was considerable – to the burgh.'